Getting Fresh

Getting Fresh

IN AND AROUND VICTORIA
The Guide to Going Organic

ELIZABETH LEVINSON

TouchWood Editions

TouchWood Editions are an imprint of Horsdal & Schubart Publishers Ltd., Victoria, BC, Canada.

Cover and book design by Public Art & Design, Victoria, BC.
Cover photography by Tania Strauss, Victoria, BC.
Kitchen courtesy of Chris and Linda Tyrrell, Victoria, BC.
Produce from Banana Belt Fine Foods, Victoria, BC.
Illustrations in the text by Pat McCallum, Victoria, BC.

We acknowledge the support of The Canada Council for the Arts for our publishing program. We also wish to acknowledge the financial support of the Government of Canada through the Book Publishing Industry Development Program (BPDIP) for our publishing activities. We also acknowledge the financial support of the Province of British Columbia through the British Columbia Arts Council.

Printed and bound in Canada by
National Library of Canada Cataloguing in Publication Data
Levinson, Elizabeth, 1958–
    Getting fresh
    ISBN 0-920663-76-1
    1. Natural foods --British Columbia -- Victoria Region.
2. Natural food restaurants--British Columbia--Victoria Region--Guidebooks. 3. Victoria Region (B.C.)--Guidebooks.
4. Cookery (Natural foods) I. Title.
    TX369.L48 2001   641.3'02'0971128   C2001-910365-4

Printed and bound in Canada

DEDICATION
For Gemma, Lizzie and Nicholas, with love

ACKNOWLEDGMENTS

With special thanks to my publishers, Pat Touchie and Marlyn Horsdal, for their keen interest in the subject of this book; to Duddy for reading the manuscript; and to Clive for leading me down the organic path.

CAVEAT

The selection of information and listings was made by the author. No financial support was solicited or accepted from any person or business included herein. The author and publishers assume no legal responsibility for the completeness or accuracy of the contents of this book. As the organic culture is constantly changing and growing, every attempt has been made to ensure that all data used were accurate at the time of publication.

Contents

Getting fresh right on your doorstep

Chapter Three: Pick of the Shops 93

Where to buy organic produce. Where to get fresh

Chapter Four: The Staff of Life 115

And other foods we can't live without

Fresh seasonal bounties from local growers and food producers

CONTENTS

The Recipes

Introduction

We all have our idea of a great Saturday morning.

One of mine is rising early to choose organic produce at the cornucopian New Duncan Farmers' Market, then meandering over to The Community Farm Store, and ending up lunching alfresco overlooking the vineyards of Vigneti Zanatta. If the mood continues (and how could it not?), I'll take a rambling tour of the Cowichan Valley's farms and vineyards in the afternoon. I arrive home with a carload of fresh organic produce, a bouquet of sunflowers, Susan Minette's cinnamon buns, loaves of Merridale House bread, maybe a couple of bottles of local wine, and the satisfaction of having been on a great gastronomic journey. During the week that follows, I can joyfully relive each stop along the way as I prepare meals from the fruits of my hunting and gathering.

Why, I have been asked, would one bother?

It can be hard to answer this without sounding preachy, without appearing to have "gone organic," and be out to convert the world. The simple answer is that I enjoy the hunt, the pleasure of discovering and purchasing organic and natural foods from the passionate people who produce them. The more didactic, yet compelling, reason is that I want to be part of the solution to the way people eat. It galls me that children are ingesting organophosphates, a class of pesticides known to cause permanent brain damage and neurological dysfunction; that workers on non-organic farms face higher rates of cancer, respiratory problems and other major diseases; and that soil and groundwater are damaged and depleted of natural biological life through intensive farming.

I'm not John Lennon, but I want everyone to give organics a chance.

So I decided to write this book, a road map of sorts, to show how prevalent organic food is in the fields, on the grocery shelves, and on restaurant tables in and around Victoria. The choice is there for everyone. It's a choice I made for the health of my family. It's a choice one can make for the sake of the environment and the future of the planet. Economically speaking, the more people who make the choice, the more affordable organics will be.

You'll find a Victoria urban gardener with sweet, juicy garlic to sell, a Salt Spring Island dairy farm producing British-style cheeses from a small Jersey herd, brown-box programs overflowing with just-picked goodness for your family, a legendary herb farm overlooking the Saanich Peninsula, a real German bio-bäcker and an irresistible choco- latier, a feast of country farmers' markets from James Bay to Mill Bay, and a Sooke restaurant that dazzles the senses with its organic menus. Everyone you'll meet is trying to get it right. You will be treated to orig- inal recipes from growers, vendors and some of the area's top chefs, and it is my belief that you will find better taste and better health at every stop along the way.

Enjoy the journey!

Chapter One: Farm Fresh

THE PLEASURE OF PICKING AND CHOOSING PRODUCE AT SOURCE

"If you have a romantic idea about being an organic farmer, you need to know what the work feels like." (Marti Martin-Wood, *Outstanding in Her Field*, a film made in 1994 about local female organic farmers)

"Nature provides the best example, so why not follow it?" (Mike Lane, Ruckle Farm)

"Feed the soil, plant enough for the bugs and eat seasonally." (Noël Richardson, Ravenhill Herb Farm)

"We just feel it's better to feed the land to feed ourselves." (Flora House, Breezy Bay Farm)

What is "Certified Organic"? "Transitional"? "Natural"? These are good questions! When you buy produce labeled "certified organic," it means the farm has been certified by a recognized, government-approved accrediting agency. In British Columbia, there are 13 such agencies. The Island Organic Producers' Association (IOPA) is responsible for certifying the farms on Vancouver Island.

The Certified Organic Associations of British Columbia (COABC) is the umbrella agency designated under the *Food Choice and Disclosure Act* to implement the British Columbia Certified Organic Program; it is the body that accredits organic certifying agencies across the province.

To become certified, a farm is put through a very rigorous conversion process for three years. During that time, the farm is classified as "Transitional," that is, the grower has applied for, and is working toward, organic certification. Farms classified as "Natural" are those using organic growing methods. Many farmers have been growing organically for years, yet have not chosen to become certified (reasons vary from "it's too expensive" to "it's not necessary; my customers know they're buying organic produce from me").

You'll find farms from all three classifications listed here. My main criterion in selecting farms for this book is that the grower has an organic conscience, and is trying his or her best to produce clean food.

ISLAND ORGANIC PRODUCERS' ASSOCIATION (IOPA)
 Contact: Peter Johnston
 Tel: (250) 333-8785
 pjohnst@island.net
 www.certifiedorganic.bc.ca
 South Island Organic Producers' Association (SIOPA), an association of Canadian Organic Growers (www.cog.ca www.cog.ca)
 Contact: Johanna Stiver (johannastiver@hotmail.com)
 or Mary Alice Johnson
 Tel: 642-3671

BABE'S HONEY FARM

334 Walton Place
RR #3
Victoria V9E 2A4
Tel: 658-8319
Natural
Honey
Owners: Babe and Charlie Warren

Farm store open year-round, Monday to Saturday, 9:30 am to 4:30 pm, Sunday, 11:00 am to 4:30 pm, holidays by appointment. Babe's Honey can be found at most Victoria area grocery stores.

Alison "Babe" and Charlie Warren have been producing honey on the Saanich Peninsula for 55 years. In spring, their bees almost cover Peninsula, Cowichan Valley and Comox Valley farms and home gardens. The Warrens credit the bees from their 2,000 hives with doing "a tremendous job of pollinating a good portion of the berries, tree fruits, vine fruits, holly, squash, pumpkins, tomatoes and other vegetables" produced in these areas.

Their bees spend summers in the logging slash areas around Port Renfrew, Lake Cowichan, and the Walbran and Carmanah valleys, where they pollinate the wildflowers, fireweed and salal, as well as the Oregon

grape and dandelions that heal barren land. This intense activity enables the plants to reproduce faster, so they can protect the soil until the reforested trees mature.

Babe believes that without her bees, "all the farmers growing organically or otherwise would get some help from hobby bees and wild bees, but not enough for a pay crop. Those tremendous fields of pumpkins are a beautiful sight in October. Thank you honey bees!"

HONEY CUSTARD

Alison "Babe" Warren, Babe's Honey Farm
Makes 6 servings.

4 EGGS, SLIGHTLY BEATEN	2 C MILK
½ C LIQUID HONEY	½ TSP VANILLA
¼ TSP SALT	

Topping

HONEY	TOASTED FLAKED COCONUT

Preheat oven to 325°F. Butter six 5-ounce custard cups. Whisk together the eggs, honey and salt. Slowly stir in the milk and vanilla. Pour mixture into the custard cups, and place cups in a pan of hot water. Bake for about 50 minutes, or until the mixture does not adhere to a knife. Serve the custard chilled or warm, topped with a drizzle of honey and toasted coconut.

NEW FOREST APIARIES

2214 Edgelow Street
Victoria V8N 1R5
Tel: 477-9834
Natural
Honey, beeswax, pollen and propolis
Owners: Cicely and Bill Spriggs

Open year-round, daily, 8:00 am to 9:00 pm. Stall at the Peninsula Farmers' Market.

Bill Spriggs has kept four hives of Italian and Carriolan bees for 24 years. His small but steady operation produces as much as 300 pounds of honey annually. Bill says his bees are "hard workers, yet have a gentle nature and are a pleasure to work with." He feels that organic

FARM FRESH APIARIES

principles must be applied throughout the honey-producing process, from pollination to extracting and bottling the honey. "Anything that comes in contact with it should be absolutely clean," he says, "so that the honey the bees produce is not altered in any way."

APPLE CRISP

Bill Spriggs, New Forest Apiaries
Makes 4-6 servings.

4 C APPLES, PEELED AND SLICED	½ C COCONUT
½ C WALNUTS OR HAZELNUTS, CHOPPED	¾ C HONEY
VANILLA ICE CREAM, WHIPPING CREAM OR YOGURT AS ACCOMPANIMENT	

Preheat oven to 350°F. Place sliced apples in a greased casserole dish and pour the honey over the slices. Mix gently to ensure all apple slices are coated with honey. Place the apple/honey mixture in the oven and bake for 30 minutes. Remove the casserole from the oven and sprinkle the coconut and nuts over the apples. Bake for a further 10 minutes. Remove the crisp from the oven, and serve either hot or cold with vanilla ice cream, whipping cream or yogurt.

Bill's note: "I feel very good about this recipe because the ingredients are, with the exception of the coconut, grown in our garden."

Author's note: A delicious alternative to crumbles that use butter. Find your own level of sweetness — ⅓ cup of honey was perfect for me.

QUAILS' ROOST FARM

4129 Happy Valley Road
Metchosin V9C 3X8
Tel: 478-1329
ptasker@telus.net
Natural
Honey, pollen and honeycomb; 30 kinds of apples from the end of September through October
Owners: Joan and Peter Tasker

Open year-round —"please call ahead." Stall at Metchosin Farmers' Market.

This small-scale operation produces a wide range of honey including arbutus, salal, blackberry, fireweed and wildflower. The beehives are maintained in different locations in Metchosin, where Joan and Peter's Blue

Orchard bees provide pollination services. Peter emphasizes that "all crops must be naturally grown, as honey bees are very sensitive to any pesticide."

TUGWELL CREEK FARM

8750 West Coast Road
Sooke V0S 1N0
Tel/Fax: 642-1956
www.tugwellcreekfarm.com
dana-l@home.com
Natural
Honey
Owners: Robert Liptrot and Dana LaComte

Open February to November, Sunday to Thursday, by appointment (or chance!) between 9:00 am and 5:00 pm. Tugwell Creek Farm Honey is also sold at West Coast Natural Foods, Sooke Regional Museum, Sooke Harbour House Gift Shop, Lifestyle Markets, Feast of Fields, in September, and the Sooke Christmas Craft Show and Creative Craft Show, in November.

On a 12-acre farm with a salmon-bearing creek running through it, and a breathtaking view of the Olympic Peninsula, Robert and Dana tend 75 beehives, raise chickens and goats, and work a large organic vegetable garden and greenhouse. Dana says they "depend on 100% organic sources of nectar and pollen for the bees, as anything less causes bee mortality and a loss in harvest." The hives are placed out where bees can forage for pesticide-free nectar from fireweed, salal, hawksbeard and pearly everlasting blossoms.

LAVENDER HONEY CHEESECAKE

Dana LaComte, Tugwell Creek Farm
Makes 8-10 servings.

½ LB PLAIN SHORTBREAD COOKIES
5 TBSP MELTED BUTTER
3 TBSP LAVENDER PETALS, TIED IN CHEESECLOTH OR LARGE TEA BALL
6 OZ TUGWELL CREEK FARM WILDFLOWER HONEY
8 OZ GOAT CHEESE OR CREAM CHEESE
1¼ C HEAVY CREAM (WHIPPING CREAM)
FRESH SPRIGS OF LAVENDER AND HONEYCOMB FOR GARNISH

Crush the shortbread cookies in food processor or with a rolling pin. Place the crumbs and melted butter in a bowl and stir until completely combined. Press mixture into a 9" springform cake pan, and refrigerate for 1 hour. Make lavender infusion by placing lavender-filled cheesecloth or tea ball, 2 tsp of the honey and 2½ tbsp hot water in a measuring cup and leave to steep for 15 minutes. Remove cheesecloth or tea ball. In a large bowl, beat together the goat or cream cheese and remaining honey until smooth, then gradually add the lavender infusion. Whip the cream until it forms soft peaks and then fold it gently into the cheese mixture. Pour the filling over the crumb base, then refrigerate for 3-4 hours. Serve the cheesecake garnished with fresh sprigs of lavender and a piece of honeycomb.

ARBUTUS BAY DEER FARMS

770 Beechwood Drive
Mayne Island V0N 2J0
Tel/Fax: (250) 539-2301
Order toll free: 1-800-514-DEER (3337)
Natural
Farmed fallow venison (Fenison™)
Owner: Paula Buchholz

Open year-round, Monday to Saturday. Phone in advance if you are coming from a distance! Fenison™ is sold from the farm or by mail order.

This is a fallow deer farm, producing tender meat with a very low (2-3%) fat content and a mild flavour, long renowned in Europe. The farmed fallow venison, which Paula has trademarked Fenison™, is a "sophisticated alternative to other red meats." Deer are fed in a natural habitat on organic hay, and their diet is free of pesticides, antibiotics, steroids and hormones.

The meat is available fresh-frozen and vacuum packed, and includes such delicacies as prosciutto of Fenison™ and filets of Fenison™ in Madeira.

Originally from Germany, Paula came to Mayne Island "to be closer to nature." She started the farm 12 years ago, and is proud to be offering organically raised meat to the North American market.

STEAKS OF FENISON™ WITH BLACKBERRIES
Paula Buchholz, Arbutus Bay Deer Farms
Makes 2 servings.

2 FENISON™ STEAKS, CUT FROM THE LEG, OR FILETS, ABOUT ½" THICK
SEA SALT AND PEPPER, TO TASTE
1 TBSP BUTTER
2 SHALLOTS, FINELY CHOPPED
½ TSP GINGER ROOT, FINELY CHOPPED
1 SMALL GARLIC CLOVE, CHOPPED
JUICE OF ½ LEMON
½ C CREAM
1 C BLACKBERRIES

Season Fenison™ steaks lightly with sea salt and pepper to taste. Melt half the butter in a heavy pan and sauté the shallots, ginger and garlic over low heat. Add the lemon juice and simmer until reduced by half to intensify the flavours. Stir in the cream. Add the blackberries and heat through, then transfer sauce to a heated bowl. Return pan to the stove and increase heat to high. Melt the remaining butter and sauté the steaks for about a minute on each side. Mix in the sauce and serve immediately over hot pasta or rice.

Paula's note: "Because the Fenison™ has no fat content, this dish is also very suitable prepared in advance to be eaten cold for a picnic. If you are looking for a simpler preparation for everyday, sauté onions and garlic, then quickly pan-fry the steaks. Bon appetit!"

OLDFIELD VALLEY OSTRICH
6260 Central Saanich Road
Victoria V8Z 5T7
Tel: 744-4419
Fax: 544-1096
hammer@pacificcoast.net
Natural
Ostrich meat
Owners: Robert and Stephanie Hammer

Open by appointment only. Direct restaurant sales.

FARM FRESH MEAT

My first encounter with ostrich was when Sean Brennan prepared it to perfection for my husband at Café Brio. Naturally, it came from local producers Bob and Stephanie Hammer, who raise the birds on their six-acre farm at the base of Bear Hill Mountain. The Hammers started their farm three years ago with two, three-month old ostriches, and now have three breeding pairs.

The eggs come with the good weather. Stephanie says they "love working with the birds," and delight in the hatching season, when as many as 22 chicks emerge from the big, hard eggs. The ostriches are raised without drugs: no hormones, antibiotics or chemicals are used, and they are processed at 12 to 14 months. The meat is exceptionally lean, with a lower cholesterol and calorie count than chicken, turkey, beef, lamb or pork.

WATER CHESTNUT MEATBALLS
Stephanie Hammer, Oldfield Valley Ostrich
Makes 75 appetizers.

> 1 LB LEAN GROUND OSTRICH MEAT
> ½ LB LEAN GROUND PORK
> 2 EGGS, SLIGHTLY BEATEN
> ¼ C DRY BREAD CRUMBS
> 1 TBSP GARLIC POWDER
> 1 TBSP SOY SAUCE
> 1 8-OZ CAN WATER CHESTNUTS, DRAINED AND FINELY CHOPPED
> 1 C TERIYAKI SAUCE

Preheat oven to 375°F. In a medium bowl, combine the ostrich, pork, eggs, salt, bread crumbs, soy sauce, garlic powder and water chestnuts. Shape into 1" balls, and arrange on a rack in a broiler pan. Bake 15-18 minutes, or until the meatballs are browned. Drain and discard the drippings. To serve, pour the teriyaki sauce into a small bowl, spear the warm baked meatballs with small wooden picks, and dip into the sauce.

RUCKLE FARM
1801 Beaver Point Road
Salt Spring Island V8K 1W3
Tel: (250) 653-4071
Natural
Lamb, beef, pork, poultry, hay, flowers, apples, vegetables and baked goods

Owners: The Ruckle Family
Managers: Mike Lane and Marjorie Clark

Farm-gate sales April to October, daily, 8:00 am to dusk. Order ahead for meat.

Henry Ruckle first settled at Beaver Point on Salt Spring Island in 1872, and eventually expanded his farm to 1,196 acres. In 1973, Gordon and Lotus Ruckle offered the province of British Columbia 996 acres and eight kilometres of shoreline to create the magnificent Ruckle Provincial Park.

The farm specializes in naturally raised, free-range livestock. There is a 100-year-old heritage orchard, with 160 of the original 600 heritage apple trees still producing fruit. The old varieties include Canada Reinette, Baldwin, Northern Spy, Tolman Sweet, Lemon Pippin, 20 Ounce Pippins, Duchess of Oldenberg and Blenheim Orange, as well as some unknown varieties that are located in the old sheep shed orchard. There is a giant pear tree, the Louise Bonne de Jersey, which stands about 90 feet tall, and five types of nuts are also grown.

Mike Lane and his family have been operating the farm for ten years, with help from the Ruckle family. The night we chatted, one of the Ruckle ladies had been down to assist with the second birthing of sheep triplets that week. Mike says simply, "It's natural to be natural," and can't imagine farming any other way. As he says, "nature provides the best example, so why not follow it?"

STONEFIELD FARM
1114 Deerwood Place
Mill Bay V0R 2P0
Tel/Fax: (250) 743-3861
Natural
Beef, pork, chicken, turkey, eggs
Owners: Pat and Brian Swan
Farm-gate sales May 1 to October 16, Tuesday to Saturday, 10:00 am to 5:00 pm, except Wednesday, when Stonefield Farm sells at a farm stand across from Kerry Park Recreation Centre on Shawnigan Mill Bay Road from 4:00 to 7:00 pm; on Saturdays, they are also at the New Duncan Farmers' Market. Call for special orders and Christmas season dates.

This is a small, diversified farm that does not use pesticides or herbicides. Pat and Brian produce naturally raised roasting chickens, turkeys,

pork, beef and eggs without the use of antibiotics. They are particularly proud of their extra-lean pork sausage line — from mild breakfast links to spicy chorizo.

Other crops are gourmet salad greens, edible flowers, bush beans, melons, garlic, onions, leeks, squash, peas, pickling cucumbers, basil and other herbs. The farm market, which is a combined effort of Stonefield Farm and two other local farms (Apple Bear Farm and Shady Brook Farm), features baked goods, homemade candies, beverages and other local products.

Direct Farm Marketing Tour

An initiative of the Southern Vancouver Island Direct Farm Marketing Association, the Direct Farm Marketing Tour offers locals a chance to visit growers and learn more about their produce. On the first Sunday in July, you can take your pick of more than 20 farms on the Saanich Peninsula, Metchosin and the Cowichan Valley. Robert Thompson has the info at 655-5656.

COWICHAN BAY FARM

1560 Cowichan Bay Road
RR #1
Cowichan Bay V0R 1N0
Tel/Fax: (250) 746-7884
www.cowichanbayfarm.com
farmer@cowichanbayfarm.com
Natural and Transitional
Pasture-raised chicken and turkey
Owners: Lyle and Fiona Young

Open by appointment or by chance — "please call ahead." Home delivery available. Direct restaurant sales. Products can be purchased in Victoria at Mattick's Farm Market, Chef on the Run and Feys & Hobbs: Catered Arts Inc.

Lyle and Fiona Young raise their birds according to their own philosophy, "live as close to nature as possible." Lyle explains that the birds are "raised in small social groups in roomy outdoor pens that protect them from predators and inclement weather. The pens are moved every day to give the birds full access to fresh grass and fresh air. We believe the chlorophyll component of the perennial grasses our birds graze daily – the salad bar – makes them the excellent eating experience and high health product they are. We encourage customers to ask if the 'free range' products they are purchasing have access to fresh grass daily."

The Youngs raise 5,000 natural pasture-raised birds a year, and are now also raising 1,500 transitional birds. Lyle says they encourage organic certification "although the pastured poultry model exceeds the minimum organic standards and addresses areas they are lacking by ensuring that fresh green grass and a clean place to eat, sleep and express natural behaviour is available every day to the pastured birds."

COUNTRY STYLE ROAST GARLIC HERB CHICKEN

Fiona Young, Cowichan Bay Farm
Makes 4 servings.

1 PASTURE-RAISED CHICKEN, 3-5 LB
FRESH THYME, ROUGHLY CHOPPED   1 GARLIC CLOVE, MINCED
FRESH TARRAGON, ROUGHLY CHOPPED   1 LEMON

Preheat oven to 325°F. Remove the giblets from the chicken. Squeeze the juice of the lemon all over the chicken and into the body cavity. Sprinkle the herbs and minced garlic over the chicken and into the cavity. Put the spent lemon into the cavity of the chicken. Place the chicken on a rack in a roasting pan, and bake for 15 minutes per pound, or until a leg easily pops out of its joint. Cooking time may vary, depending on size of bird, and whether or not convection is used.

Fiona's note: "Guard against overcooking!"

LEE'S HILL FARM

120 Lee Road
Salt Spring Island V8K 2A5
Tel: (250) 653-9188
Certified Organic
Pastured poultry
Owner: Tom Pickett

Home delivery of chickens and eggs, some farm-gate sales — "please call ahead."

Tom Pickett says his interest in organic farming stems back to reading copies of *Mother Earth* and *Hammersmith* in the cold city winters. He and his daughter finally made the switch to Salt Spring Island, where he experimented with market gardening and raising pigs. Eventually, he turned to poultry raising and now runs a 3½-acre poultry farm. His daughter helps out with the chickens, although "she preferred the pigs."

The decision to become certified was based on "believing in the organic principles and wanting to produce clean food, raised and dispatched in a humane fashion." Tom runs his birds on grass, changing their location several times a day.

SHADY BROOK FARM

1055 Cheeke Road
Cobble Hill V0R 1L0
Tel: (250) 743-7055
shadybrook@home.com
Natural
Pasture-raised chicken, turkey and egg layers
Owners: Steve and Dodie Miller

Open by appointment. Stall at the New Duncan Farmers' Market.

The Millers' 11-acre farm south of Duncan has never been treated with pesticides or chemical fertilizers. Their birds are pasture-raised, but they do come inside at night for protection from the raccoons. They receive "all veggie" feeds and no medications. Steve says, "We raise all our birds from day-old chicks, and we do our processing in co-operation with a neighbour, in his provincially-inspected facility. We have complete control of the health and quality of our poultry from start to finish."

The chickens are available from May through November, and average four to five pounds each. They may be purchased whole or in parts. The turkeys are raised for Thanksgiving and Christmas, and must be ordered early as demand is great and quantities limited. Eggs are from brown-laying varieties such as Harco and ISA-Brown. Steve attributes the beautiful bright orange yolks to the chickens' access to lots of fresh air and fresh greens.

THE POULTRY RANGE
3570 Telegraph Road
Cobble Hill V0R 1L0
Tel: (250) 743-4816
Fax: (250) 743-4840
Natural
Turkeys and chickens
Owners: Richard and Carol Ewing

Farm-gate sales May 1 to December 23, Monday to Saturday, 10:00 am to 4:00 pm. Products sold at specialty food stores and to "the best gourmet restaurants, and most discerning farm-gate customers."

On Richard and Carol Ewing's property, one acre is dedicated to chickens and three acres to turkeys. The turkeys receive medicated feed for the first four weeks until their immune systems are developed, then they go on to a non-medicated vegetable formula. The chickens are raised from birth on non-medicated vegetable formula, and never receive antibiotics or growth hormones.

Richard says their philosophy is "to raise the best product we can and we accomplish this by giving our birds outside runs, access to sand and grit, clean bedding, fresh water, heat when necessary and continuous access to good quality feed. Our butchering facility guarantees us one of the best end products on Vancouver Island."

Orchards and Fruit Farms

"He conducted her about...the fruit-garden and green-houses, where he asked her if she liked strawberries. "Yes," said Tess, "when they come." (*Tess of the D'Urbervilles*, Thomas Hardy)

And don't we all prefer to eat our fruit in season?

APPLE LUSCIOUS ORGANIC ORCHARD
110 Heidi Place
Salt Spring Island V8K 1W5
Tel: (250) 653-2007
www.appleluscious.com
burtonh@saltspring.com
Certified Organic
Apples
Owners: Harry Burton and Debbie McNamara

Open most days through the year, except the month of January (call to ensure they are home).

Harry is not only an enthusiastic organic grower, he's an enthusiastic promoter of the Salt Spring Island orchard scene and its spectacular Apple Festival in October (see Harry's website). The festival showcases some 15 orchards — most of which are producing organic apples — and over 350 varieties grown on the island! You can spend the day touring the orchards and sampling the fruit, which is served straight from the trees, pressed into cider and baked by the indomitable Salt Spring Women's Institute into over 200 pies.

Apple Luscious itself grows over 175 apple varieties on five acres, including 20 red-fleshed varieties. Using only manure, seaweed, fish waste and hay mulch, this "wild" orchard does minimal mowing and no irrigation. Varieties include Cox's Orange Pippin, Northern Spy, Jonagold, Gravenstein, Belle de Boskoop, King, as well as many unusual ones. Harry and Debbie insist that if you don't say "that's incredible" at least once when you taste their fruit, they have not been successful.

Harry says, "It's important to the future of the world that we return to the organic food production of our ancestors. This is especially important to children. So it gives me joy to produce great-tasting organic apples. Because our orchard is wild, other vegetation, such as weeds and blackberries, grow nearby. This tends to help to balance and maximize the insect, bird and snake populations. It is a great joy to see all these creatures and know the orchard is also a healthy home for them."

BLACKBERRY APPLE CRISP
Harry Burton and Debbie McNamara, Apple Luscious Organic Orchard
Makes 6-8 servings.

5-6 APPLES, CORED AND SLICED (PEELING OPTIONAL)
2 TSP FRESHLY SQUEEZED LEMON JUICE (OPTIONAL)
2-3 C RIPE BLACKBERRIES (FRESH, OR FROZEN AND THAWED)
¾ C BROWN SUGAR (NOT PACKED)
1 C ROLLED OATS
½ C FLOUR (WHOLE WHEAT OR UNBLEACHED)
2 TBSP UNBLEACHED FLOUR
1 TSP CINNAMON
½ C BUTTER OR MARGERINE

Preheat oven to 325°F. Spread sliced apples in an 8" square baking dish and sprinkle with lemon juice (to prevent browning). In a medium bowl, mix blackberries gently with the 2 tbsp flour, and spread mixture over apples. In a medium bowl, mix the ½ c flour, rolled oats and cinnamon, and cut in butter or margerine until crumbly. Sprinkle the crumble mixture over the blackberries, and bake for 50-60 minutes.

Harry's note: "Makes a great potluck offering!"

BLUEBEARY HILL FARM

5927 Oldfield Road
Victoria
Mailing address: 5926 Bear Hill Road, Victoria, V9E 2J3
Tel: 652-0641
Natural
Blueberries
Owners: The Bull Family

U-pick with your own containers mid-July to late August; picked berries available at the farm gate, days vary throughout the season. After July 10, call for a recorded message on the picking schedule.

Donna Bull has always loved blueberries, so when the family moved to Bear Hill and acquired a one-acre property down the road, blueberries were the obvious crop, and Bluebeary Hill Farm was the obvious name. As no one else was growing unsprayed blueberries around there, the Bulls have always had a popular operation. Donna (like Bertolt Brecht before her) believes "you are what you eat!" and she enjoys shopping from the farm gates in her rural neighbourhood, and knowing how her family's food is grown.

FARM FRESH ORCHARDS AND FRUIT FARMS

Donna involved her children from the beginning, to "teach social skills and give them an awareness of what they eat, and what's available." Now teenagers, they often run the u-pick operation themselves.

Every year the family helps Donna develop a new blueberry recipe for customers. The following is a particular favourite.

BLUEBERRY OATMEAL MUFFINS

The Bull Family, Bluebeary Hill Farm
Makes 12 muffins.

½ C ROLLED OATS*	1½ C FLOUR
½ C FRESH SQUEEZED ORANGE JUICE	1½ TSP BAKING POWDER
½ C BUTTER	½ TSP BAKING SODA
½ C SUGAR	½ TSP SALT
2 EGGS	1 C FRESH OR FROZEN BLUEBERRIES

Topping

2 TBSP SUGAR	1½ TSP CINNAMON

*Donna uses quick cooking oats

Preheat oven to 400°F. Grease 12-cup muffin pan. In a mixing bowl, combine the rolled oats and orange juice. Stir well and set aside. Cream butter and ½ cup of the sugar together, add the eggs and beat until light and creamy. Stir oat and orange mixture into butter mixture. In another bowl, combine the dry ingredients: flour, baking powder, baking soda and salt. Mix dry ingredients into butter mixture. Fold in blueberries (if using frozen berries, be sure to keep them in the freezer until you need them or your batter will turn purple!). Spoon muffin mixture into muffin cups. Combine topping ingredients and sprinkle on top of muffins. Bake approximately 15 minutes, until golden on top.

FERN CREEK FARM

492 Isabella Point Road
Salt Spring Island V8K 1V4
Tel/Fax: (250) 653-9158
cleitch@saltspring.com
Natural
Apples, pears and plums
Owners: Craig Leitch and Beverley Stewart

Open every day, 7:30 am to 8:00 pm.

Originally the Hamilton homestead, this property was first planted in 1897. From its glorious location on the ocean at Fulford Harbour, the farm is now a family-owned and -operated heritage orchard. There are about 30 old apple trees producing 25 varieties including Transparent, Canada Reinette, Golden Russet, Blenheim Orange, Red Delicious, Wismer's Dessert, Gravenstein, Baldwin, Ben Davis, Mother (of New York State), Ben Davis, Newton Spitzenberg, Alexander, Wolf River, King of Tompkin's County, Millionaire, Yellow Bell Flower, Fall Pippin and Triumph de Boskoop.

Pear trees yield Anjou, Bartlett, Bosc and Winter Nellis; plums grown include Victoria, Imperial, Greengage and Italian Prune; and there are cherries (Bing, Queen Anne), walnuts, hazelnuts and sweet chestnuts.

Craig has always grown organically, but doesn't favour certification, feeling it is an unnecessary process that "pushes prices up." He "enjoys bringing completely organically grown fruit and produce to the public (no sprays, no fertilizers whatsoever) at a very reasonable cost."

FRESH APPLE CAKE
Craig Leitch and Bev Stewart, Fern Creek Farm
Makes 1 loaf-shaped cake.

> 4 C FRESH APPLES, CUT INTO ¼"-½" CHUNKS (WOLF RIVER APPLES WORK BEST)
> 1¼ C RAW CANE SUGAR, BROWN OR WHITE
> 1 C WALNUTS, CHOPPED
> ¼ C VIRGIN OLIVE OIL
> 2 EGGS, BEATEN
> 1 TSP VANILLA
> 2 C WHOLE WHEAT FLOUR
> 1 TSP NON-ALUM BAKING SODA
> 1 TSP CINNAMON
> PINCH OF SEA SALT

Preheat oven to 350°F. Grease and flour a 4" x 9" loaf pan. Place the apple chunks in a large mixing bowl. Add the sugar and walnuts, and mix well. Add the oil, eggs and vanilla, and mix again. In another bowl, mix together the dry ingredients. Make a well in the centre of the wet mixture, and add the dry ingredients. Mix well. Using a spatula, scrape cake batter into the loaf pan, and bake for approximately 1 hour.

FARM FRESH ORCHARDS AND FRUIT FARMS

ISABELLA FARM

300 Holmes Road
Salt Spring Island V8K IT6
Tel: (250) 653-9634
Fax: (250) 653-4485
Certified Organic
Apples
Owner: Ian Franey

Open by appointment — "please call ahead." Produce sold at local organic shops, at market, to individuals as well as to shops in Victoria when quantities permit. These include Capers Community Market, Lifestyle Markets and Thrifty Foods.

Isabella Farm was a peach and apple orchard during the 1970s and early 80s, before it was transformed into a certified apple orchard. The Franey family grows over 20 new and heritage varieties on about 220 trees, on a secluded, south-facing farmstead at Isabella Point. Their bounty includes Jonagold, Jona Free Liberty, Prima, Spartan, Gala, Cox, Gravenstein, Tydeman, Mutsu, Red Free, Newton, Rome Beauty and Northern Spy.

Ian says, "Our aim is to provide the freshest, healthiest, best tasting fruit possible. It must be untainted, free of any artificial pesticides, herbicides or fertilizers. Grown with care and respect for the environment, and human health, nurtured with the aid of beneficial insects, an organic apple a day keeps the doctor away!"

BRANDIED BUTTERSCOTCH APPLES

Ian Franey, Isabella Farm
Makes 4 servings.

1 C BROWN SUGAR	1 TBSP CORNSTARCH
½ - ¼ C WATER	1 TBSP BUTTER
3 C TART APPLES, SLICED	½ TBSP VANILLA EXTRACT
¾ C MILK	3 TBSP BRANDY
A FEW GRAINS OF SALT	

In a large saucepan, combine the brown sugar and water. Heat to the boiling point. Add the apples, then cover and boil gently until tender. Carefully remove apples from syrup. Place the apples in a serving bowl, or in 4 sherbet glasses. In a medium saucepan, blend together the milk, salt and cornstarch. Cook slowly, stirring constantly

until the boiling point is reached. Add the syrup in which the apples were boiled, and cook 3-4 minutes longer. Remove from heat, and add the butter, vanilla and brandy.

Pour the brandied butterscotch sauce over the apples, dividing equally between sherbet glasses. Serve hot or cold.

Author's note: Depending on your taste for brandy, you may wish to sample the sauce after adding the first or second tablespoon. My family loved it after two!

SWALLOW HILL FARM AND ORCHARD

4910 William Head Road
Victoria V9C 3Y8
Tel/Fax: 474-4042
www.swallowhillfarm.com
info@swallowhillfarm.com
Natural
Apples, Asian pears, blueberries and rhubarb
Owners: Peter and Gini Walsh

Open daily during growing season, otherwise by appointment — "please call ahead." Stall at Metchosin Farmers' Market.

The Walshs' four-acre hobby farm includes an acre of orchards with some 300 trees growing Belle de Boskoop, Cox's Orange Pippin, Fuji, Jona Free, Jonagold, Prima, Red Free, Red Gravenstein, Royal Gala, Summer Red and several other apple varieties.

The property was once part of a pioneer farm belonging to Hans Lars Helgesen of Norway, who settled there in 1863 because it reminded him of his previous farm overlooking the Oslo Fjord. The Walshes were equally taken with the beautiful land and ocean view, and bought it in 1987. They share their good fortune with laying hens, ducks, sheep, two miniature horses, and a much-loved border collie, all of which delight guests at the farm's charming bed and breakfast.

Gini says they believe in natural farming methods, using "integrated pest management (IPM) to let natural predators control the pests." They "sell the apples straight off the tree with no worry about chemical residue."

FARM FRESH ORCHARDS AND FRUIT FARMS

APPLE GINGER JAM

Gini Walsh, Swallow Hill Farm

Makes about 8 cups.

> 1 C GINGER ROOT, FINELY CHOPPED (OR MORE OR LESS TO TASTE)
> 5-6 LARGE APPLES (TART-SWEET CRISP ONES SUCH AS PRIMA OR JONAGOLD),
> CORED, NOT PEELED, AND FINELY CHOPPED BY HAND OR IN FOOD PROCESSOR
> 2 C APPLE JUICE OR WATER
> 6 C SUGAR
> 1 TSP POWDERED GINGER (OPTIONAL)

Microwave Method

In a large deep casserole or other microwave container, combine ginger root and apple. Stir in liquid (juice or water). Cook on high heat in microwave until all is tender, approximately 40 minutes. Add sugar and stir well until sugar dissolves. Cook again on high heat for at least 20-30 minutes or until jam stage* is reached. Add powdered ginger and stir. Let jam cool completely before ladling into freezer containers; then seal containers and freeze. Alternately, seal jam in hot sterile jars.

Stovetop Method

In a large jamming pan or Dutch oven, combine the ginger root and apples. Stir in liquid (juice or water). Cook over high heat until the fruit is tender. Stir regularly during cooking. Remove from heat and add the sugar. Stir well until the sugar dissolves. Return to heat, bring to a boil, stirring constantly to avoid burning. Once boiling point is reached, reduce heat to simmer and cook for another 20-30 minutes or until jam stage* is reached. Add the powdered ginger and stir. Let cool completely before ladling into hot sterile containers and seal.

Gini's note: "I created the first batch without measuring. I liked the jam, but it wasn't gingery enough for my taste, so I decided to make a second batch, adding more ginger and being careful to record all measurements for the sake of your readers! There's no need to add pectin, as apples are high in natural pectin, so this jam sets easily."

GINI WALSH DESCRIBES THE "JAM STAGE"

The "jam stage" is universally recognized to be 220°F, but that can vary. To be absolutely certain the jam is set, Gini Walsh also uses the spoon test. "When the jam sheets off a spoon it has reached the 'jam stage.' My cookbook describes this as follows: 'Dip a cool metal spoon into boiling jam. When the jam stage is reached, the liquid will not flow off the spoon in a stream, but will divide into distinct drops that run together and fall off the spoon as one sheet.' Most jam-makers will know this and will recognize the appearance."

WHIMS FARM

130 Primrose Lane
Salt Spring Island V8K 1C1
Tel: (250) 537-5403
Natural
Apples
Owners: Bob and Judy Weeden

Open August to November, by appointment.

Bob and Judy, former professors from Alaska, bought this 17-acre farm in 1988. It was originally part of the homestead of the Whims, one of the early black families who settled on Salt Spring in 1860.

Today, the farm boasts 25 century-old fruit trees and 175 new fruit trees, with 138 heritage varieties of apples including Wagener, Snow, Golden Russet, Ashmeads Kernel, Pound Sweet, Fall Pippin, The Lady, and Cornish Gilli Flower. Bob's hobby is collecting heritage varieties, especially those grown on Canada's west coast before 1900. He says The Lady is one of his prized finds, being thousands of years old. While Bob tends the orchard, Judy pots; her stoneware and porcelain artworks are on display in the farm's gallery.

Bob grows by strictly organic methods, even eschewing allowed bug suppressants, and says it is "essential to go that way all over the world." He sees no reason why that cannot happen, but feels the main hurdle will be "the transition from huge mono-cultures to mixed farms."

YELLOW POINT ORCHARD

2786 Gwens Lane
Ladysmith V9G 1C1
Tel: (250) 245-3180
arthur_jordan@telus.net
Natural
Apples
Owners: Art and Bobbi Jordan

Farm-gate sales in September and October by appointment. Stalls at the New Duncan Farmers' Market and Cedar Farmers' Market.

Art and Bobbi grow unsprayed Freedom, Liberty and Nova apples on 300 dwarf apple trees. Because the trees are so small, they occupy only a small portion of the family's four-acre property. If the crops allow,

FARM FRESH ORCHARDS AND FRUIT FARMS

the Jordans also have Jonagold and Fuji apples, apple chutney and candy apples for sale, and you'll always find a basket of discounted windfalls available at their stall for baking.

Daughter Jennifer, who takes a keen interest in the orchard and helps her father at the markets, says, "It's important to watch what goes into our bodies — we need to avoid cancer-causing sprays at all costs."

MINCEMEAT

Bobbi Jordan, Yellow Point Orchard
Makes 16 cups.

> 4 LB APPLES (ANY TYPE), PEELED, CORED AND CHOPPED
> 3 C BROWN SUGAR
> 1 C JELLY OR JAM SUCH AS PLUM OR BLACKBERRY
> 1 LB CURRANTS, SCALDED*
> 3 LB RAISINS, SCALDED*
> 2 C APPLE JUICE**
> ¼ C APPLE CIDER VINEGAR
> 1 TSP EACH OF SALT, CLOVES, ALLSPICE, NUTMEG AND CINNAMON
> ½ TSP MACE
> 1 CAN CRUSHED PINEAPPLE
> 1 LB GLAZED PEEL (EITHER CANDIED FRUIT OR CITRON, OR A MIXTURE OF BOTH)
> GRATED RIND OF 2 ORANGES
> GRATED RIND OF 2 LEMONS

*To scald the currants and raisins, place them in a bowl and pour boiling water over. Let sit for 5 minutes, then drain.

** Bobbi uses 1 c apple juice and 1 c brandy

Blend all ingredients in a large pan and simmer for approximately one hour or until the apples are soft and mushy. Spoon mincemeat into jars and store in refrigerator or seal in a hot water bath and store in a cool place.

Vegetables and Herbs

ALM* ORGANIC FARM
3680 Otter Point Road
P.O. Box 807
Sooke V0S 1N0

Tel: 642-2131, 642-3671
Fax: 642-3671
alm@islandnet.com
* from the Arabic letters signifiying beginning, middle and end
Certified Organic
Vegetables, herbs and fruit; seeds
Owner: Mary Alice Johnson

Not open to the public. Box-program orders and minimum $20 pre-orders only at the farm. Direct restaurant sales. Stall at Moss Street Market. Seed sales through Full Circle Seeds.

Owner Mary Alice Johnson, a former schoolteacher and President of the Canadian Organic Growers, now parlays her love of teaching and knowledge of organic farming into the Stewards of Irreplaceable Land (SOIL) and Willing Workers on Organic Farms (WWOOF) programs. Over 50 apprentices from countries including China, Germany and Japan have learned to garden from the soil up at ALM Organic Farm. Mary Alice also teaches organic gardening with Tina Fraser (Lynburn Farm) at Camosun College.

A sign in the farm's pumpkin patch reads, "Work is love made visible," and the evidence of love is everywhere, from the delicate seedlings being nurtured for planting, to the homemade jams and jellies stacked up in the cold house, ready to be tucked into wooden boxes along with just-picked produce for 20 local families subscribing to the farm's box program.

Mary Alice is an experimental farmer, always looking for new things to grow. The day I visited she had given Shady Lane natural ice cream manufacturers some Mexican epazote, an herb that aids digestion and prevents flatulence. The resulting ice cream was going to be served at a chili bake-off in Victoria. ALM supplies Sooke Harbour House, Re-Bar, The Empress Room and The Marina Restaurant, and Mary Alice enjoys a fruitful exchange with the chefs; a new vegetable from her farm often inspires a new dish, just as a chef's request for a rare herb can lead to its appearance in Mary Alice's greenhouse.

ALM Organic Farm occupies half of Sooke's original 20-acre Harris farm which was established in 1910. Only four acres are cultivated. "We reside as lightly on the land as possible and sell locally, feeding ourselves and our community," says Mary Alice. "The least amount of interference with our natural environment the better."

SPICY PUMPKIN PIE

Mary Alice Johnson, ALM Organic Farm
Makes 8-10 servings.

PASTRY FOR A 10" PIE

1 SMALL PUMPKIN	1 TSP CINNAMON
1 C SUGAR	1 TSP GINGER
1 C BROWN SUGAR	¼ TSP CLOVES
1 TSP SALT	¼ TSP ALLSPICE
1 TSP NUTMEG	4 EGGS

¼ C BUTTER (OPTIONAL)
WHIPPED CREAM WITH MAPLE SUGAR OR SYRUP (OPTIONAL)
CHEESE (OPTIONAL)

Preheat oven to 450°F. Cut pumpkin and remove seeds (leave the skin on). Cut into large pieces, and place in steamer. Place steamer in two inches of water in the bottom of a large covered pan, and steam until pumpkin is soft. Drain and cool. Remove skin which will come off easily after cooking. Mash pumpkin and combine with sugars, spices and eggs. You may add melted butter at this time if you want a richer pie. Pour into the uncooked pie shell, and bake for 10 minutes. Reduce heat to 350°F and bake for another 40 minutes or until the centre is set (test by inserting a knife into the centre — if it comes out clean, the pie is set). Cool pie and serve with the sweetened whipped cream and cheese, if desired.

BENSONS' OLDE TYME FARM

2409 Yellow Point Road
Nanaimo V9X 1W5
Tel/Fax: (250) 722-3526
gb_benson@hotmail.com
Natural
Vegetables, herbs, garlic and flowers
Owners: George and Betty Benson and Sons

Farm-gate sales May to October, Wednesday to Saturday, 10:00 am to 7:00 pm. Call ahead to pick up at other times; deliveries available. Stall at Cedar Farmers' Market and New Duncan Farmers' Market.

The Benson farm was originally a dairy. In 1994, the family cultivated four acres, originally to produce natural food for themselves. George Benson says, "Our natural philosophy and our #1 Metchosin soil blended well, and our vegetables actually did grow!"

They began selling from the farm gate, then at the Cedar Farmers' Market, and now also supply to the Good Food and MING (Mid-Island Natural Growers) green box progams, and, at harvest time, they have a stall at the Duncan market.

George says they "have always believed you are what you eat. We have taken courses and read materials over the years on farm development, and we have our own 'heritage' family members to direct us. We use only old-time farming equipment, and use nothing in the soil or on the crops that we wouldn't eat ourselves! All family members help with the chores and hold positions in farm organizations that are in line with our natural food philosophy."

HARVEST SALAD

Copied to fly

Betty Benson, Bensons' Olde Tyme Farm
Makes 4 servings.

Salad

1 MED CAULIFLOWER, CUT INTO BITE-SIZED PIECES
1 LG BROCCOLI, CUT INTO BITE-SIZED PIECES
4 STEMS (INCLUDING GREENS) BOK CHOY, SLICED THINLY
4 CARROTS, SLICED THINLY
1 MED YELLOW ZUCCHINI, CUT INTO BITE-SIZED PIECES
1 LG CUCUMBER, CUT INTO BITE-SIZED PIECES
1 LG TOMATO, CUT INTO WEDGES
1 LEEK (WHITE ONLY), SLICED FINELY
CHOPPED CILANTRO AND BASIL

Dressing

¼ C OLIVE OIL
2 GARLIC CLOVES*
2 TBSP LIME JUICE

1 TBSP BROWN SUGAR
3 TBSP SOY SAUCE

*Betty favours Bensons' Russian Rocumble garlic

In a large bowl, mix together all of the salad ingredients. Combine the dressing ingredients in a blender or food processor, and process on high until well blended. Pour the dressing over the vegetables and toss to coat. Garnish with a generous sprinkling of cilantro and basil.

BENTBACK FARMS

180 Durrance Road
Victoria V9E 2A3
Tel: 544-1028
Fax: 544-1030
scampper@telus.net
Certified Organic
Herbs and vegetables
Owner: Sid Bartlett

Open on weekends in summer, 10:00 am to 4:00 pm.

Bentback Farms have been owned by the family for some 40 years. Located in the Highlands, the 32-acre property includes treed areas, hayfields, and an organically certified acre of vegetables. In addition to soil crops, tomatoes, peppers, basil and herbs are grown in the greenhouse.

Sid Bartlett is the present generation owner of the farm, and he had no trouble receiving certification two years ago, as his farming methods had always been organic.

Sister Violet Leclair is currently turning an occupation into a vocation with an on-site wheat-free bakery. "Our entire family is allergic to wheat, so I've always baked wheat-free cakes, pies and bread, using organic tapioca, rice and potato flours," she says. Violet has previously sold her baked goods to naturopaths, and is looking forward to welcoming the public to her bakery. She believes that growing and eating organic foods is "the only way to keep healthy!"

HERBED TURKEY CASSEROLE

Violet Leclair, Bentback Farms
Makes 4 servings.

2 TSP SALT, OR TO TASTE
2½ TBSP FLOUR
2 TBSP BASIL
1 TSP SUMMER SAVORY
3 LB TURKEY BREAST, SKIN REMOVED AND BONED
BUTTER FOR SAUTÉING
1 C LONG GRAIN BROWN RICE
1 C ALMONDS, SKINS ON, ROUGHLY CHOPPED OR LEFT WHOLE
½ LB DOMESTIC MUSHROOMS, SLICED OR LEFT WHOLE

3 TBSP DICED ONION
2 C TURKEY OR CHICKEN BROTH
1¼ C WHITE WINE

Preheat oven to 350°F. In a bag large enough to hold the turkey breast, mix together the salt, flour, basil and summer savory. Put the turkey breast in the bag and shake to coat. Heat butter in a large skillet, then brown the turkey breast all over. Spread the rice on the bottom of a baking dish and place the turkey on top of the rice. Add the almonds, mushrooms and onions on top of the turkey. Mix together the broth and wine and pour over casserole. Cover and bake for approximately 1½ hours.

BREEZY BAY FARM

131 Payne Road
Saturna Island VON 2Y0
Tel: (250) 539-5200
Fax: (250) 539-5201
www.saturnaherbs.com
saturnaherbs@canada.com
Certified Organic
Culinary herbs
Owner: Saturna Freeschool Community Projects Ltd.

No set times: "Anyone can stop by the farm and find someone to help them, or just look around."

The 25-acre Breezy Bay Farm is located in a sheltered valley on Saturna Island. The property is mainly forest with approximately ten acres in pasture for sheep together with greenhouses and an acre in cultivation, where Flora House and other members of the Saturna Freeschool Community Projects (SFCP) grow organic culinary herbs. The SFCP was named for a freeschool that was operated on the property in the early 1970s. Flora says, "Since then the farm has been run by members and a number of 'newcomers,' that is, you've only been on Saturna for 20 years or so!"

All drying and packaging of the herbs is done on site, and they are sold through the farm's website, and at the local general store on Saturna. I order by mailing a downloaded order form, and the herbs arrive within the week.

Flora says the farmers "don't have a 'philosophy' per se, we just feel it's better to feed the land to feed ourselves. We have farmed this way for over 25 years, although we are new to 'certification'."

HERB ROASTED BABY POTATOES
Flora House, Breezy Bay Farm

> 1-2 LB SMALL RED POTATOES
> ½ C OLIVE OIL
> 3 CLOVES GARLIC
> 1 TBSP DRIED OR ¼ C FRESH BASIL

Preheat oven to 350°F. Wash the potatoes, then halve or quarter depending on size. Place potatoes in a single layer in a large baking dish. Crush the garlic and mix it with the olive oil and basil. Pour herb mixture over the potatoes and stir to coat thoroughly. Bake for 1½ hours or until the potatoes are golden.

Flora's note: "Rosemary can be substituted for basil — you just don't need as much."

CHARMAN FARMS
5914 Pirates Road
Pender Island V0N 2M2
Tel: (250) 629-6559
www.gulfislands.com/charmanfarms
charmanfarms@gulfislands.com
Natural
Vegetables, particularly garlic
Owners: Dan and Kae Charman
Not open to the public. Produce is sold at the Pender Island Farmers' Market and at the Pender Island Community Hall, May to October.

With approximately two acres in cultivation, Charman Farms specializes in organically grown garlic that is sold in bulk and braids, as well as pickled. There are vegetables in season, goat cheese, yogurt, and eggs. Dan and Kae have been the proud recipients of the Pender Island Fall Fair Vegetable Trophy for five years running.

Dan believes in "low volume, high quality, intensive labour. Enrich the soil, sustain agriculture, and be paid enough to be able to continue to feed Mother Earth, who in turn feeds and enriches us."

LEMON CHÈVRE WITH ROASTED GARLIC

Kae Charman, Charman Farms

Chèvre

4 LITRES FRESH GOAT MILK*
JUICE FROM 2 LEMONS
½ TSP SALT (OR TO TASTE)

*fresh goat milk is available from most large grocery stores and health food stores

In a pan on top of the stove, bring the milk to 186°F to pasteurize (or until the surface skins). Remove from heat, cover, and let cool to 100°F (or just above room temperature). Add the lemon juice to the milk. Stir, then allow mixture to "harden" for one hour. Add salt, then pour into cheesecloth and hang to drain (if you catch the whey that drains out, it can be used in bread recipes). When the mixture has drained for 4-6 hours, transfer it from the cheesecloth to a bowl and refrigerate.

Garlic

4 WHOLE HEADS GARLIC
PINCH OF SALT

Preheat oven to 375°F. With a sharp knife, slice the tips off the garlic heads, and place them in a shallow baking pan or garlic baker. Sprinkle with salt. Bake 30-40 minutes until soft. Serve the Lemon Chèvre with the Roasted Garlic on crackers or heavy dark bread.

Kae's note: "No extra oil is needed — garlic is full of its own oil!"

COWICHAN VALLEY ORGANIC FARM

6182 Lakes Road
Duncan V9L 4J5
Tel: (250) 748-8089
Fax: (250) 748-8089
davewieb@island.net
Certified Organic
Vegetables, herbs, greenhouse crops, fruit, flowers and nuts
Owner: Dave Wiebe

Open by appointment. Supplies restaurants and a couple of local box programs.

ave runs a nine-acre farm situated on the outskirts of Duncan, with one acre of field crops and one commercial greenhouse in production. He says he has "lots more room and plans to expand." He started farming three years ago "for environmental reasons," and is a strong advocate of community-supported agriculture. He wholesales his produce to local box programs specifically because they are local. Dave is also a director of the Island Organic Producers' Association (IOPA).

CUCUMBER CORNER

6220 Welch Road
Saanichton V8M 1W7
Tel: 544-4831
Fax: 544-4066
e-lanthony@home.com
Natural
Cucumbers, dill, green beans, beets, snow peas, English peas and sugar snap peas
Owners: Earle and Lorna Anthony

Open daily, approximately June 15 to September 15, approximately 9:00 am to 6:00 pm. Call ahead for cucumber and dill orders (available August to mid-September).

This family-owned and -operated 3½-acre hobby farm has been the Anthonys' retirement project since 1996. At their roadside stand, the main crop for sale is peas, but the farm's bounty, and the owners' passion, is pickling cucumbers.

Lorna feels that "the agencies which regulate the use of pesticides have not fully evaluated the long-term impact of introducing these chemicals into the soil and environment. Therefore, we do not use pesticides, herbicides or insecticides. Our practice is to combat pests by crop rotation, cultivation and biological pests."

GRANDMA'S DILL PICKLES

Lorna and Earle Anthony, Cucumber Corner
Makes 7 1-quart jars.

7 LB PICKLING CUCUMBERS
FRESH DILL
21 CLOVES GARLIC

7 GRAPE LEAVES
6 C PICKLING VINEGAR
11 C WATER
¾ C COARSE PICKLING SALT

Clean cucumbers gently, ensuring the blossom is removed. Soak in ice water while making the brine.

Brine

Combine and bring to a boil the vinegar, water and salt. Into each sterilized jar, place 1 bunch dill, 2 or 3 cloves of garlic and cucumbers. Pour in hot brine, leaving ½" space from top of jar. Remove air bubbles by puncturing with a knife. Wipe rim, screw on sterilized lids (follow manufacturer's instructions). Process for 5 minutes in hot water bath*. Wait six weeks before eating!

*The Bernardin Guide to Home Preserving (1995) recommends heat-processing in a boiling water canner for 10 to 15 minutes to ensure a seal and to prevent spoilage from organisms such as surface yeast and molds.

Lorna's note: "The secret to good pickles is to process them within 24 hours of the cucumbers having been picked."

LORNA ANTHONY'S TIPS FOR MAKING GREAT PICKLES

Approximately one pound of pickling cucumbers fill a one-quart jar. Wash cucumbers well and ensure the blossom is removed, as it contains an enzyme that will prevent the cucumber from staying crisp.

White vinegar should be between 5-7% acetic acid (labelled "pickling vinegar").

Follow closely the instructions that accompany the brand of lids you are using.

If garlic cloves turn bluish green, this is not a concern. It can be due to the type of cookware used or the garlic's pigment reacting with the vinegar.

DUCK CREEK FARM

134 Tripp Road
Salt Spring Island V8K 1K5
Tel: (250) 537-5942
Fax: (250) 537-5220
duckcreek@saltspring.com

Certified Organic
Garlic, basil, cucumbers, potatoes, apples, squash, hay and a few wild turkeys, laying hens, and feeder lambs (raised naturally but not for certified sale)
Owners: John and Lynda Wilcox and Family

Open by appointment only, produce sold daily in spring and summer through the Growing Circle Food Co-op in Ganges.

Duck Creek Farm is a certified bio-dynamic organic family farm. It covers 15 acres of the upper valley of Duck Creek, which runs from St. Mary's Lake to Duck Bay at the sea, north of Vesuvius on Salt Spring Island.

Close to one fifth of the farm has been set aside for conservation, and the Wilcoxes hold a water rights habitat conservation licence on the creek as well as a two-acre-foot irrigation licence for garden plots. John says they happily "co-exist with the beaver who provides us with in season sub-irrigation to the garden plots. In return we do fish and wildlife habitat creation and conservation work." In future the family hopes to work with interested parties to create a nature trail through the forest along the creek on the farm.

John is a long-time proponent of ecosystem stewardship and planning, and pens a monthly viewpoint for *Country Life*, the province's farm newspaper. He believes in "stewarding the whole system, not just its parts. Feed the soil, not the plant, practise community not commodity agriculture, work first of all toward a shared local economy with affordable permanent tenures in the land and recognize wealth and returns on investment to be more than just monetary. Ensure quality work and products from the farm to the public. Work toward an open countryside venue and respect all forms of life."

POTLUCK CARROTS
John Wilcox, Duck Creek Farm
Makes 2-6 servings.

1 BUNCH CHANTENAY CARROTS (OR SIMILAR)
BUTTER
MAPLE SYRUP
WALNUTS, TOASTED

"Slice up the carrots
into pencil thin strips, then

steam 'til they're tender but crisp.
Melted butter brushed on
In a heat (covered) pot, and
Add maple syrup then too
(not much 'cause they're sweet;
adjust measure to suit).
Next, sprinkle on toasted walnuts.
Now cover the lot to serve piping hot
And give to a potluck from you
or sweet as a dinner for two!"*

*rhyming by John

John's note: "This pretty simple vegetable dish tastes great!"

WHAT IS BIO-DYNAMIC FARMING?

Another good question!

"This is what our troubled time needs more than anything else — only then will we be able to look into a better future." (Ehrenfried E. Pfeiffer, *An Introduction to Bio-Dynamics*)

John Wilcox of Duck Creek Farm, who practises bio-dynamic farming, describes it as "a whole-systems approach to farming that reduces the inputs to focus on the farming system itself, not the products." It is a method of ecological agriculture that is practised and recognized worldwide.

Bio-dynamics grew out of anthroposophy, the spiritual science articulated by Rudolf Steiner, an Austrian-born philosopher, in 1924. He had been approached by a group of European farmers trying to solve the problem of soil decline. His holistic approach to agriculture "notes the interrelationship of all kingdoms — mineral, plant, animal and human — and their intricate correspondence to the rhythms and activities of the larger cosmos."* Bio-dynamic farming follows Steiner's ideals of self-contained farms, community-supported agriculture, quality over quantity, treating the soil as a live element, and close observation of nature.

* from *What is Biodynamics?* by Sherry Wildfeur at www.biodynamics.com

Contact: Bio-dynamic Agriculture Society of British Columbia
4895 Marshall Road
Duncan V9L 6T3
Fax: (250) 748-4287

FARM FRESH VEGETABLES AND HERBS

EISENHAWER ORGANIC PRODUCE
4266 Happy Valley Road
Victoria V9L 3Y1
Tel: 474-7161
deisenhawer@pacificcoast.net
Transitional*
Beans, beets, carrots, tomatoes, raspberries, squash, kale, potatoes, mesclun mix and more
Owner: Dieter Eisenhawer

Farm-gate sales year-round, Wednesday and Sunday afternoons, 12:00 noon to dusk. Stall at Metchosin Farmers' Market and Moss Street Market. *The farm was Certified Organic in 1990, but that status changed after the 1999 aerial gypsy moth spraying. Dieter is confident that his farm will regain certification next year.

When I think back, it was probably Dieter's famous mesclun mix with its abundant herbs that sold me on the huge difference in taste between conventional and organic produce. Seriously, chlorophyll had never tasted so good.

When Dieter left carpentry to get away from the dust and chemicals, he began to grow and eat organically, and attributes his new lifestyle to having cured his chronic bronchitis. "I believe in living a healthy life, free from pesticides, herbicides, fungicides, antibiotics and GMOs (genetically modified organisms)," he says. "None of these are inherent in nature, so why would I want to eat them?"

In addition to his farm-gate and market sales, Dieter provides a customized winter box service to six to eight families in Victoria. He stores root vegetables and apples, just like my own grandfather used to, in a root cellar, and cautions those planning to do the same "not to store apples with potatoes, as gas emitted from the apples encourage the potatoes to sprout."

Dieter also harvests seeds from over 24 vegetables, of which his mesclun mix, arugula, beans, lettuces and tomatoes are the most popular. He bemoans the fact that people aren't interested in his Schwarz Wurzel seeds, which Dieter says produce a black root vegetable known in Europe as "the poor man's asparagus" because when the roots are peeled after cooking, they taste very similar.

An active member of the Association for the Preservation of Rural Metchosin, Dieter describes himself as "one of a very outspoken group of

people against whatever creeps around the Metchosin border and threatens the natural habitat of this rural community."

ELK LAKE FARM

700 Linnet Lane
Victoria V9E 2Bl
Tel: 479-7773
Natural
Kiwi (end November), Prima apples (early September), produce, Cindy's Country Fruit Products
Owner: Cindy Stark

Not open to the public. Phone ahead for custom orders or see Cindy at Moss Street Market.

Cindy Stark has farmed organically for 16 years, and enjoys taking her produce and homemade chutneys, dipping sauce, dessert sauces, kiwi sorbet and pure apple fruit bars to market.

She believes that "food is a basic necessity for survival. We are increasingly aware that naturally occurring vitamins and minerals can help to ward off disease and cancer, increasing life span. Studies have shown that organically grown foods have a much higher percentage of nutrients. I believe that poisoning food and the environment with chemicals and fertilizers is simply not logical."

ENGELER FARM

4255 Trans Canada Highway
RR #1
Cobble Hill VOR lL0
Tel: (250) 743-4267
Fax: (250) 743-8367
ffcfisle@island.net
Natural
Mixed farm: vegetables and herbs, meat and poultry, vineyard
Owners: Mara Jernigan and Alfons Obererlacher

Call ahead for farm-gate sales. Stall at Frayne Centre Market and New Duncan Farmers' Market.

FARM FRESH VEGETABLES AND HERBS

If ever there was a diverse and sustainable farming operation, Engeler Farm ("farm of the angels") is it. On their 5.4-acre mixed farm, Mara Jernigan and Alfons Obererlacher raise rare breeds of goats, sheep and pigs; supply local restaurants with pastured chicken and Muscovy duck; grow a market harvest of veggies, herbs and salad greens; and produce two acres of Pinot Noir and Pinot Gris grapes which are sold to BC wineries (the last harvest went to Glenterra Vineyards). They also offer farm tours for groups of 6 to 20, cooking classes and eclectic special events such as bat-watching parties. When guests of the exclusive Aerie Resort want to see something of the area, Mara and Alfons take them on customized tours of local farms followed by lunch alfresco at Engeler Farm. They also represent Summerhill Wines on Vancouver Island, and Mara is the Island Representative for Farm Folk/City Folk.

"We believe in growing top quality, nutritious, fresh produce by growing without herbicides or pesticides," says Mara. "As a former chef, I enjoy producing as much of our own food as possible and enjoy experimenting with heirloom and heritage varieties."

A new wood-burning brick oven and major kitchen expansion this spring will allow Engeler Farm to offer an even greater range of food-related classes and demonstrations. Call ahead to find out what's planned, or to book a private event.

CHICKEN BRAISED IN BEER WITH LEEKS, BACON, CHANTERELLES AND FRESH SAGE

Mara Jernigan, Engeler Farm
Makes 4 servings.

1 LARGE, 3-5 LB CHICKEN*
4 TBSP ALL-PURPOSE FLOUR
SALT AND PEPPER
2 TBSP OLIVE OIL
1 C LEEKS, WHITE PART ONLY, SLICED LENGTHWISE AND DICED
2 TBSP GARLIC, CHOPPED
1C FRESH CHANTERELLE MUSHROOMS, CUT IN HALF OR QUARTERED
¼ C SMOKED BACON, DICED
1 C CHICKEN STOCK
1 C MICROBREW STOUT OR ALE
¼ C WHIPPING CREAM
4 TBSP FRESH SAGE LEAVES, CHOPPED

*Mara recommends using pastured or free-range chicken

Preheat oven to 375°F. Cut the chicken into 8 equal-sized pieces, bone in, to yield the following: 2 thighs, 2 drumsticks, 2 breast tips, 2 breast bases with wingettes (you can reserve the neck and backbone to make stock). Roll the chicken pieces in the flour seasoned with salt and pepper. Save seasoned flour mixture. In a large, braising, oven-proof frying pan (with tight-fitting lid), heat the olive oil. Sauté the chicken pieces all over — skin side down first — until seared golden brown. Remove the chicken and set aside. Add the leeks, garlic, mushrooms and bacon to pan, season with salt and pepper, and lower heat to prevent browning. When the leeks are translucent, add a bit of the beer to deglaze the pan. Stir with a wooden spoon to avoid any lumps caused by the flour on the bottom of the pan. Add the remaining beer, bring the mixture to a simmer and add the chicken. Cover pan and place in oven for approximately 35 minutes. Check the legs of the chicken with a knife to make sure the juices run clear. If it is properly cooked, remove the pan from the oven. Remove the chicken, and place pan back on the stove at a simmer. Skim 2 tbsp of chicken fat from the top of the sauce, combine with the remaining flour in a small saucepan, and mix well. Add about ½ c of the sauce to this and mix again. Pour all of this slurry back into the sauce and mix well. Add the sage and cream to the sauce, and simmer for about 5 minutes to cook out any starchy flavour. Taste for seasoning (adjust with salt and pepper as necessary), add the chicken to the sauce, heat and serve.

FARM FOLK/CITY FOLK

"Something happens to people who plant seeds — it is impossible to watch a plant grow and flourish without getting a sense of the miracle of all life." (Herb Barbolet, Co-founder, Farm Folk/City Folk)

Farm Folk/City Folk is leading the way toward "food security for everyone." This non-profit society advocates a collaborative approach between the agricultural and food sectors to ensure that "people eat local, fresh, seasonal foods, grown using farming practices that contribute to the health of the planet."

The society provides education and networking opportunities; supports a number of gardening projects including Linking Land and Future Farmers (LLAFF) that matches people who want to farm but don't have land with landowners who don't farm; and organizes public awareness events such as the exuberant Feast of Fields. This annual celebration of the fall harvest brings together the growers, vendors and chefs, and the many beneficiaries of their efforts. In addition to great food, good wine and collegiality, the event raises funds to support Farm Folk/City Folk's programs.

FARM FRESH VEGETABLES AND HERBS

Farm Folk/City Folk "speaks out for BC food and agriculture at all levels of decision making," including presenting a significant brief in 1999 to the BC government's Select Standing Committee on Agriculture and Fisheries regarding an Agri-Food Policy for British Columbia.

Vancouver Island Contact: Mara Jernigan

Tel: (250) 743-4267

Fax: (250) 743-8367

www.ffcf.bc.ca

ffcfisle@island.net

FOREST SPRING FARM

9028 East Saanich Road
Sidney V8L 1H5
Tel/Fax: 655-FARM (3276)
www.zanichelligarlic.com
garlic@islandnet.com
Certified Organic
Garlic, vegetables and berries
Owners: Patrick and Dianne Zanichelli

Farm gate open August to October, Saturdays, 10:00 am to 2:00 pm. The garlic is sold through Fresh Piks, and at Capers Community Market and Peninsula Co-op. The seed garlic is sold by Integrity Sales, Dig This and Buckerfields.

Dianne Zanichelli laughs as she describes the farm's "humble beginning." "We put in a garlic patch measuring 15 by 20 feet, and planted the first crop upside down!"

The Zanichellis have it more than well figured out now. Every year, they plant 75,000 seeds on 1½ acres. Three fields are used for rotation, and the soil is replenished with six cover crops, compost from the farm and wild fish fertilizer. Water for the crops comes from an artesian spring that provides up to 7,000 gallons of water per day. They designed their own planter that enables two people to sit and plant 4,000 cloves an hour. The harvester that they also designed lifts the plants for easy removal. A Herculean harvest takes place in July, when family and friends help bring in the garlic, and students are hired to grade and bundle. After curing in the 100-year-old barn, the garlic is processed for market.

Pat says they grow garlic for its high oil and nutrient level. "In May, we sell garlic greens. In August, the cured garlic destined for the market is ready. Seed garlic is cured differently and longer and is available in September. Nothing is wasted as the stalks from the garlic are fed to a neighbour's cows and the loose skins and roots are fed to a neighbour's sheep."

Forest Spring Farm also produces vegetables, herbs, wild blackberries, dahlias, old-fashioned flowers and dried flowers, as well as five old varieties of strawberries (including the British Sovereign which was grown on the Saanich Peninsula from the 1930s to 50s).

SAANICH SALMON BARBEQUE

Patrick and Dianne Zanichelli, Forest Spring Farm
Makes 10-20 servings (1½ - 2 lb salmon fillets serves 4).

1½ C SOY SAUCE	2 TBSP EXTRA VIRGIN OLIVE OIL
2 CLOVES GARLIC	5-10 LB SALMON FILLETS
4 TBSP GINGER ROOT	½ TSP FRESHLY GROUND PEPPER

Garnish

½ C CHIVES, CUT FINE WITH SCISSORS
2 TBSP BUTTER

Blend and refrigerate the chives and butter for garnish. Pour soy sauce into a 9" x 12" baking dish. Grate garlic and ginger root into soy sauce, add olive oil and mix together. Place salmon fillets in the baking dish, turning several times to coat. Add more soy, if needed, to cover fish. Grind fresh pepper over salmon, and cover dish. Refrigerate for 2 hours, turning salmon at least twice. Prepare the barbeque, preferably using aged maple, and cook when maple is reduced to coals. If using gas, heat barbeque to high temperature. Place fillets in barbeque "toaster" racks. Depending on the thickness of the fillets, cook 3 to 4 minutes each side. Take care not to overcook. When fish is ready, gently separate the rack and place whole fillets on a platter. Garnish with the chive butter. If smaller pieces are desired, cut fish while in the rack.

TUSCAN BAKED HALIBUT

Patrick and Dianne Zanichelli, Forest Spring Farm
Makes 4 servings.

4 POTATOES, SLICED THIN
1 WHITE ONION, CHOPPED FINE
1 CLOVE GARLIC, SLICED THIN OVER THE SALT WHICH WILL SOAK UP THE GARLIC'S OIL

FARM FRESH VEGETABLES AND HERBS

1 TSP SALT
½ TSP FRESHLY GROUND PEPPER
2 SPRIGS ITALIAN PARSLEY
1 TSP ROSEMARY, COARSELY CHOPPED
1½ TBSP ANCHOVY FILLETS, CHOPPED
¼ C EXTRA VIRGIN OLIVE OIL
2 LB HALIBUT FILLETS

Preheat oven to 375°F. Layer half of the sliced potatoes in the bottom of a buttered 9" x 9" baking dish. Sprinkle half of the onion, garlic, salt, pepper, parsley, rosemary, anchovies and olive oil over the sliced potatoes. Place halibut fillets on top of the seasoned potatoes, skin side down. Cover the fish with the remaining potatoes and seasonings. Bake for 35 minutes.

Dianne's note: "You may wish to replace the parsley and rosemary with chopped fennel or tarragon and 2 tbsp grated ginger root."

PAT ZANICHELLI SHARES "A LITTLE PRACTICAL AND
PHILOSOPHICAL THOUGHT ON CURING SEED GARLIC"

"At Forest Spring Farm, the freshly harvested garlic is hung over ropes stretched between cedar trees in our forested area. The forest canopy provides shade and cover from any light summer rain, and the ebb and flow of the warm summer sea breezes provides gentle drying of the fresh moisture-laden garlic.

"After a few weeks, this seed garlic is hung on the south and west side of our 100-plus-year-old barn. The sun heats the barn's porous walls which serve to slowly draw the moisture from the garlic bulbs. A constant breeze moving through the barn ensures a warm, dry curing process. By early September, the seed garlic has reached a dry, nut-like hardness which is ready for planting the first week in October.

"Our seed garlic is graded to provide the optimum size for nutrition and robustness. Its ability to endure the adversity of our recent wetter-than-usual winters and provide garlic high in oil and nutrient values bodes well for our crops. I believe we are drawn to use the plants that thrive through adversity, as they in turn assist us in dealing with whatever adversity life may bring."

FRISS FARM

6666 West Saanich Road
P.O. Box 457
Brentwood Bay V8M 1R3
Tel: 652-8422
Natural
Owners: Leo and Leona Friss
Vegetables, herbs, fruit and free-range eggs

Open year-round, daily from 9:00 am to 6:00 pm. Stall at Saanich Peninsula Market.

Leo Friss says he and his family "take pride in the ecological and organic approach to producing healthy, pesticide-free homegrown quality produce." The evidence is in the veritable cornucopia at their farm gate and stall at the Saanich Peninsula Market: strawberries, marionberries, loganberries, beans, broccoli, cauliflower, cabbage, beets, carrots, cucumber, Super Sweet and Peaches 'n Cream corn, garlic, lettuces, onions, peas, leeks, spinach, Swiss chard, potatoes, rhubarb, peppers, tomatoes, various squash and zucchini, parsley, mint, basil and chives.

VEGETABLE MEDLEY

Leona Friss, Friss Farm
Makes 4 servings.

2 TBSP OLIVE OIL
2 CLOVES GARLIC, CHOPPED
1 TBSP GINGER ROOT, CHOPPED
1 C ONIONS, CHOPPED
1 C CARROTS, CHOPPED
1 C ZUCCHINI (GREEN OR YELLOW), CHOPPED
1 C MUSHROOMS, SLICED
1 PEPPER (RED, YELLOW OR GREEN OR ⅓ OF EACH), SLICED INTO THIN STRIPS
1 SMALL EGGPLANT, CUT INTO PIECES
1 14-OZ TIN TOMATOES
1 TBSP BASIL, CHOPPED

In a large sauce pan or Dutch oven, sauté garlic and ginger in the olive oil. Add the remaining vegetables, season with salt and pepper and simmer on low heat for appoximately 2 hours.

Leona's note: "This dish can be served alone, or with rice or your choice of pasta."

GABRIOLA GOURMET GARLIC
1025 Horseshoe Road
RR #1, Site 5P, C95
Gabriola Island V0R 1X0
Tel/Fax: (250) 247-0132
www.gabriolagourmetgarlic.com
gabriolagourmetgarlic@home.com
Natural
Garlic and garlic products
Owner: Ken Stefanson and Llie Brotherton

Farm-gate sales every day during daylight hours. Stall at Gabriola Farmers' Market, Cedar Farmers' Market and New Duncan Farmers' Market. Also available at the Silva Bay market on Gabriola Island in July and August.

Ken and Llie grow about 3,000 pounds of nine types of garlic in three different locations on the island. Their largest crops are Russian Hard Neck, Porcelain and Purplestripe. When fully grown, Ken says the crops stand four to five feet high, and he is always delighted to show them off.

Says Ken, "Everything is grown without chemicals. We feed our hens organic feed, and do our best to keep our air clean, our water pure. It's only natural that what we ingest should be as natural as possible."

Ken sells fresh garlic, garlic seed and his own garlic chutney, cured garlic, pickled garlic and hot pickled garlic (a new recipe that he says he is finally happy with!).

GAVIN'S FRESH HERBS
1550 Mills Road, West Saanich
Mailing address: #2-7847 East Saanich Road, Saanichton, V8M 2B4
Tel: 652-6558
Natural
Fresh herbs
Owner: Gavin Hanson

Not open to the public (yet!). Direct restaurant sales to The Empress Room, The Aerie Resort, Café Brio, Ocean Point Resort, Sunflower Café, The Latch, and many others.

Gavin has always gardened, but 16 years ago, he began to grow in earnest. Some property became available on an old dairy farm nearby, so he went to work carving a spectacular, circular herb garden out of the brush and weeds. Protectively nestled beside an old barn, Gavin's plants grow in his own compost in raised beds created from rocks.

Why circular? "My former garden was on a city lot, and I had to walk 200 feet from one part to the next. The circle is more compact, and focuses energy on the plants." The fresh-herb business started in the summer of 1984, when exceptionally warm weather had given him a bumper crop of basil. He took the surplus to The Empress Hotel, and was off and running from there.

Gavin grows his herbs outdoors "because one gets a more robust, flavourful product than in a greenhouse. The oils in the herbs become more developed outdoors, and that means better taste." He has never used chemicals "because they're expensive and they deplete the soil."

Gavin delivers his herbs, edible flowers and flower sprigs directly to local restaurants and hotels. He also grows salad greens which he delivers to ten lucky locals each week. Eventually, he would like to sell at the farm gate, but in the meantime, he welcomes visitors to his special garden.

HILLSIDE FARM

1748 Mt. Newton Cross Road
Saanichton V8M 1L1
Tel: 652-0650
Natural
12 varieties of winter squash, strawberries, raspberries, rhubarb, broad beans, scarlet runner, pole beans and year-round free range, antibiotic-free eggs
Owners: Joanne and Tad Stoch

Farm gate open May to October, Wednesday and Saturday, 9:00 am to 6:00 pm.

Graphic artist Joanne Stoch and her husband Tad, a printer, found the perfect lifestyle six years ago at Hillside Farm. Tad had grown up on the family farm in Poland, where natural growing methods were used. Says Joanne, "We wanted to offer people home-grown produce picked the same day, produce that was hand planted and weeded, and free of chemicals. It's healthier, tastes better, and can be less expensive."

The Stochs grow naturally on two acres, using no pesticides or herbicides other than a minimum amount of soap or organic solutions. And, just as animals worked on the family farm in Poland, Joanne is training her small draft horse to help with light plowing and harrowing.

Joanne is a member of the Farm Marketing Association and takes an avid interest in natural farming methods. She believes there can be a middle ground in organic farming, and is convinced there is a higher concentration of chemicals in people's suburban gardens than on local farms. She offers tours for young children to put them in contact with "the entire cycle" of life on a farm.

KILDARA FARMS

11293 Chalet Road
Sidney   V8L 5M1
Tel: 655-3093
Fax: 655-3040
kildara@pacificcoast.net
Certified Organic
12 varieties of apples, strawberries, about 50 different vegetables including 15 to 20 types of salad greens for their gourmet salad mix, winter hardy turnips, parsnips, brussels sprouts, leeks, kale and chard; eggs, lamb, roasting chickens and pork available by order.
Owners: Brian and Daphne Hughes

Open year-round, Fridays, 8:00 am to 12:00 noon. Box program delivered to drop-off points throughout Victoria on Wednesdays and Thursdays, or pick up at the farm on Friday mornings.

Brian and Daphne Hughes left the proverbial rat race 13 years ago, and never looked back. Instead they look out, from their 30-acre property, over tranquil Deep Cove, and, as Daphne says, "We feel good that we are eating better ourselves and doing our little bit for changing the world."

With ten acres cultivated, ten acres in grazing and three greenhouses, the Hughes are kept busy. Most of their produce goes into a vital box program that caters to over 200 families in and around Victoria.

Brian explains that they run the farm "on an holistic basis with a large variety of produce and including animals to make it a sound ecological unit starting with high quality, healthy soil rich in nutrients. The combination of animal waste as a basis for compost making and the use of cover crops makes for healthy produce coming from a vibrant soil."

PESTO
Daphne Hughes, Kildara Farms

> 2 C BASIL OR ITALIAN PARSLEY, OR COMBINATION OF BOTH
> 4-6 LARGE GARLIC CLOVES, PEELED
> ½ C OLIVE OIL
> 2 TBSP WALNUTS
> ⅔ C PARMESAN

Put the basil or parsley (or combination of both) in food processor. Add the other ingredients and process until mixture is smooth. Serve over pasta.

Daphne's note: "This pesto is also good on fresh bread with sliced tomatoes and some goat cheese. It's also good with roast chicken. It keeps in an airtight container in the refrigerator for approximately two weeks, or freeze in ice cube trays and use one cube at a time."

KILRENNY FARM
1470 Cowichan Bay Road
RR #3
Cobble Hill V0R 1L0
Tel: (250) 743-9019
Natural
Vegetables and herbs
Owners: Russel and Deborah Fahlman

Open from May or June to November, daily, dawn to dusk. Stall at Frayne Centre Market.

Music drew me to the tomato greenhouse, where Deborah Fahlman literally popped out from behind a plant to greet me. She and Russel have worked 1½ acres on their property for 12 years now. They grow a wide variety of vegetables that are sold in the charming on-site produce and craft shop. Herb plants are available starting in May, and free-range turkeys can be ordered for Thanksgiving and Christmas. Farm-raised roasting chickens and lamb are also on the menu.

Deborah says they use organic growing methods to "protect the local and global environment, and for great taste and better health."

GREEK BEAN SALAD
Deborah Fahlman, Kilrenny Farm
Makes 4 servings.

Salad

1 LB YOUNG GREEN BEANS
1 LB YOUNG YELLOW BEANS
SALT AND PEPPER, TO TASTE
¾ C CRUMBLED FETA CHEESE
¾ C TOASTED SLIVERED ALMONDS

Dressing

4 TBSP WHITE WINE VINEGAR
2 TBSP FRESHLY SQUEEZED LEMON JUICE
4 CLOVES GARLIC, MINCED
6 GREEN ONIONS, FINELY CHOPPED
½ C FINELY CHOPPED MINT LEAVES
½ C FINELY CHOPPED BASIL LEAVES
2 TBSP FINELY CHOPPED FRESH OREGANO
½ C OLIVE OIL

In a bowl, combine dressing ingredients and set aside. Bring a large pot of water to the boil, and cook all the beans until tender crisp (3-5 minutes). Drain the beans and immediately cool in a bowl of ice water. When cool, thoroughly drain the beans. Mix the dressing with the beans, and add salt and pepper. Sprinkle the feta cheese and slivered almonds over the salad, and toss when ready to serve.

LYNBURN FARM

Saanich
Tel: 658-4921
tjfraser@islandnet.com
Certified Organic
Seasonal produce
Lessee: Tina Fraser

Not open to the public. Tina sells her produce at Moss Street Market, to Café Brio, and through Saanich Organics box program.

Tina Fraser is a wonderful role model to many in the local farming community. She is a fifth-generation family farmer from Ontario, who had a market gardening business back east before settling in Victoria where she has studied horticulture and started her own farm. She grows vegetables on four acres that include two large greenhouses, and a fig and apple orchard.

Tina tells me her interest in growing organically was reinforced by many visits to Berkeley's Chez Panisse where she discovered the new market cuisine of Alice Waters. When Alice presented her with a bowl of delicious, just-picked, organic cherry tomatoes to eat, her passion for "nutritous, beautiful, small-scale growing" was heightened and her vocation confirmed. Tina enjoys farming on the west coast, where she "appreciates the seasons, even though it means working year-round!" She particularly enjoys her collaboration with Sean Brennan of Café Brio because he "really loves food and is always interested in trying new varieties on his menu."

Tina has been president of the South Island Organic Producers Association (SIOPA) for many years, and is a founding member of Moss Street Market and Linking Land and Farmers (LLAFF). She and Mary Alice Johnson of ALM Organic Farm have worked together for these organizations over many years, and are now inspiring a new generation of organic growers.

MAKARIA FARM

4468 Cowichan Lake Road
Duncan V9L 6J8
Tel: (250) 748-2854
makaria@home.com
Transitional (T3)
Strawberries (June to September), produce, free-range eggs and chicken
Owners: Randy and Debbie McLeod

Farm-gate sales June to September, daily, 9:00 am to 5:00 pm. "Please order ahead for eggs and chicken."

Randy and Debbie McLeod always wanted a piece of land on which to grow their own food. Six years ago their dream came true and, after experimenting with various produce and livestock, they settled on a half-acre field of strawberries as their main crop. Debbie is delighted that they are able to feed themselves and their family from the farm.

The McLeods take an ecological and organic approach to producing healthy, pesticide-free, home-grown quality food. With children and grandchildren to think about, Debbie says, "We do it to maintain a healthy earth and healthy bodies."

ZUCCHINI TOMATO STIR-FRY

Debbie McLeod, Makaria Farm
Makes 2-4 servings.

1 TBSP OLIVE OIL
6 CLOVES GARLIC, CRUSHED
1 ONION (PREFERABLY RED), THINLY SLICED
3 TOMATOES, DICED
3 ZUCCHINI, GRATED OR SLICED INTO ¼" THICK CIRCLES
1 TBSP SEASONING SALT, OR TO TASTE

Heat the olive oil in a skillet over medium high heat. Add the crushed garlic, stir and sauté. Add the sliced onion, stir and sauté. Add the diced tomatoes and sauté until the juice from the tomatoes runs out. Add the grated or sliced zucchini, and stir until tender. Add the seasoning salt, to taste. Stir, and serve when vegetables are cooked but not too soft.

MARTHA'S GARDEN

949 Lawndale Avenue
Victoria V8S 4C9
Tel: 598-7286
barchyn@island.net
Natural
Garlic, dried beans, squash, greens such as arugula, chard and kale, mesclun and herbs; vegetable and herb plants
Owner: Martha Barchyn

Open by appointment. Martha also sells at Moss Street Market.

Take a right here, and another right over there, and you find yourself in a charming private organic garden, lovingly tended by Martha Barchyn. To be on Martha's weekly email list is to eat well.

Although Martha says she is "too small to be certified," she rigorously follows the IOPA guidelines, and utilizes permaculture concepts like livestock (chickens) and native habitat (hedgerows) in her garden. She aims to "provide habitat and food for urban dwellers including insects, reptiles, birds, domestic creatures and humans. And — most importantly — to inspire others to grow their own food!"

Martha has gardened to feed her family since her early 20s when she turned a parking lot into a garden. Her children helped her in the garden when they were small, because she believes it's important for them

to know where food comes from. Today, daughter Emily cares for the family's friendly English chickens, feeding them a purely organic diet, with lots of greens from the garden.

PASTA WITH RICOTTA AND GREENS
Martha Barchyn, Martha's Garden
Makes 4 servings.

2 TBSP OLIVE OIL
4 CLOVES GARLIC
4 C LOOSELY PACKED GREENS (ANY COMBINATION OF SPINACH, KALE, CHARD, MUSTARD), WASHED, STEMS REMOVED AND CHOPPED
1 C RICOTTA CHEESE
SALT AND PEPPER TO TASTE
¼ C SUNFLOWER SEEDS
¼ C GRATED WHITE GRACE CHEESE*
ENOUGH COOKED PASTA FOR 4 SERVINGS

*made by Moonstruck Organic Cheese, or substitute any good quality white Cheddar

Mince the garlic cloves and sauté in the olive oil. Add the chopped greens to the garlic and cook gently on low heat until the greens are wilted. Add the ricotta cheese, salt and pepper, and heat through. Serve sauce over cooked pasta, topped with the sunflower seeds and grated White Grace cheese.

Martha's note: "This recipe is easy to make and illustrates what I believe: eat what we grow and produce locally (greens, garlic and cheese)."

MISTY HOLLOW FARM
2100 Bear Hill Road
Saanichton V8M 1X7
Tel: 652-0668
Fax: 544-0903
eileenl@pacificcoast.net
Natural
Seasonal produce and eggs
Owners: Eileen and Eliot Lowey

Farm-gate sales in summer, Wednesdays and weekends, day time.

This family-owned farm has ½ to ¾ of an acre in cultivation, depending on the season. The Loweys grow seasonal fruit and vegetables to feed themselves and to sell at the Moss Street Market.

Eileen Lowey says they grow organically in order to "improve and sustain the soil and to eliminate contaminants from the food and the food chain." They strive to "create balance and harmony with all living things."

The family gives back in many ways, including working with youth on the farm to train them and offer a supportive and healing environment.

BASIL VINAIGRETTE DRESSING
Eileen Lowey, Misty Hollow Farm

EQUAL PARTS WHITE BALSAMIC VINEGAR AND COLD PRESSED OLIVE OIL
FRESH BASIL, TO TASTE
FRESH GARLIC, TO TASTE

Either blend all ingredients in the blender (makes a beautiful bright green dressing), or chop the garlic and other herbs and whisk them into the olive oil and vinegar.

Eileen's note: "For variety, substitute fresh arugula, cilantro or oregano (for a Greek style dressing) in place of the basil."

PHOENIX FARM
5480 West Saanich Road
Victoria V9E 2G1
Tel: 479-5829
Certified Organic
Bedding plants and early greens in spring; cucumbers, artichokes, tomatoes, celery, herbs in summer; greenhouse crops through November; eggs year-round
Owner: Barbara Belknap

Farm-gate sales May and June, September to November, weekends, 10:00 am to 4:00 pm, July and August, Tuesday to Saturday, 10:00 am to 4:00 pm.

The phoenix at Phoenix Farm is the soil itself, which "rises" from the floods every year. Seriously, half the farm lies in a flood plain that

drains seasonally and leaves behind the rich fertile soil in which the farm's root and forage crops thrive. On higher ground, Barbara Belknap devotes four acres to pasture for the 100 laying hens and herd of pure-bred Nubian goats. Also in this area is a greenhouse and 1½ acres of market garden, from which come greens, herbs and vegetables.

Barbara and family have "been growing organically now for almost ten years. Our belief is that sustainable organic agriculture is not just a trend, but an imperative. Likewise, we feel that quality nutrition is inescapably linked to organic practices and should not be out of reach to low- or middle-income families. Produce purchased direct from Phoenix Farm is available at wholesale prices," says Barbara. "That's our way of making it work."

RAGLEY ORGANIC FARM
5717 East Sooke Road
Sooke V0S 1N0
Tel: 642-7349
Fax: 642-1946
ragley5717@aol.com
Natural
Vegetables, chickens and eggs, fresh homemade bread, pies, muffins and preserves
Owner: Josephine Hill

Farm market open April through October, Saturday and Sunday; "please call ahead for hours."

At Ragley, buying organic produce can be an historical event. The original 160-acre estate was named after the ancestral home of Lady Emily Walker, who came to East Sooke in 1912 with her husband, the Reverend Walker, and their five children. Lady Emily was a daughter of Lord Seymour, Marquess of Hertford. A previous family member was Lady Jane Seymour. The original house, which is still standing today, included a billiard room for Lady Emily on the top floor and a back staircase for the servants who accompanied them from England. It was Lady Emily and her children who eventually did most of the farm work as the servants married and left. Around 1927, she set up the East Sooke Farmers' Institute, and many of its meetings were held at Ragley.

Today the farm is 30 acres, with one acre cultivated, eight acres in pasture, and the rest treed. Barnes Creek runs along one boundary and

provides water for irrigation. There are still approximately ten of the old apple trees remaining, with the most prolific producer being an Ontario apple.

Josephine Hill is a woman with sentiments similar to Emily's, believing that "growing organic was the only choice. It became more and more apparent that the food we were being sold was not about nutrition." She credits her parents "for providing us with fresh vegetables as we were growing up. There was always a large garden. When I had children, I naturally was concerned about nutrition and food supply. Out of this grew a desire to share real food with friends and neighbours. I believe that I have a responsibility to continue to grow and make available the best possible food to those who are concerned about their food supply. It's about feeling good and doing the best you can."

LEMON CRUSTED CHICKEN

Josephine Hill, Ragley Organic Farm
Makes 4 servings.

1 CHICKEN, 3-5 LB
JUICE OF 1 OR 2 LEMONS
1 MEDIUM ONION
1 TSP OREGANO
¼ C EXTRA VIRGIN OLIVE OIL
SALT AND PEPPER, TO TASTE

Cut chicken in half or into pieces. Put onion, lemon juice, oregano, olive oil and salt and pepper into food processor and process until very well chopped. Marinate the chicken for at least one hour in the onion-lemon mixture. Preheat oven to 350°F. Put chicken into a flat roasting pan, spreading the onion-lemon mixture over the top, and bake for 1 hour and 15 minutes or until well done. The onion on top should be brown and crispy.

REBECCA'S ORGANIC GARDEN

Saanich
Tel: 652-8499
rjehn@islandnet.com
Certified Organic
40 varieties of vegetables, some berries, seeds, herbs and flowers
Lessee: Rebecca Jehn

Not open to the public. Rebecca's produce is sold at Moss Street Market, to two restaurants, and through Saanich Organics box program.

Rebecca leases one acre of land on a ten-acre farm. Her organic garden is fenced "to keep the resident deer from devouring the crops" and there is a large greenhouse in which she grows heritage tomatoes and exotic peppers. She grows "according to IOPA guidelines using compost, crop rotation, companion planting, green manure cover crops and mulch," and believes it's important to "disturb nature as little as possible, leaving the garden ecosystems more intact to support a healthy soil and garden environment. I grow a large number of my own seeds, completing the cycle of regeneration."

CHERRY TOMATO SALAD
Rebecca Jehn, Rebecca's Organic Garden
Makes 4 servings.

1 LB CHERRY TOMATOES (MIXED COLOURS AND VARIETIES ARE BEST)
½ C BASIL LEAVES
3-4 CLOVES GARLIC
1 TBSP OLIVE OIL
¼ TSP SALT

Wash and de-stem the cherry tomatoes, then slice in half lengthwise and put into a bowl. Peel and clean the garlic cloves, then mince garlic finely and add to the sliced tomatoes. Remove stems from the basil and pick clean. If necessary, wash the basil leaves, spin and pat dry to remove excess water. Chop the basil finely and add to the garlic-tomato mixture. Add the olive oil and then the salt. Toss to mix and serve at room temperature.

Rebecca's note: "It is important to serve at room temperature, as refrigerating tomatoes destroys their flavour and texture."

REDWING ORGANIC FARM
Saanichton
Tel: 544-4369
redwing@islandnet.com
Certified Organic
Vegetables, tomatoes (especially heirloom) and berries
Owner: Renana (RJ) Fisher

FARM FRESH VEGETABLES AND HERBS

Open by appointment only. Some sales made from the farm at individual request — "please call ahead." Produce available through Saanich Organics box program; stall at Moss Street Market; supplier to Camille's (yes, those are her tomatoes!).

Renana does all the farming on her ¾-acre garden by hand, without machinery of any kind. She believes that "growing organic produce is an ecologically sustaining activity and system that not only doesn't deplete the soil, but builds it and helps it become healthier and support more life. I use compost and mulch instead of tilling with machinery to simulate as natural a system as possible. I've witnessed organic farming directly result in healthier soils, ecosystems and a much stronger sense of community."

Renana, together with Robin Tunnicliffe of Llewellyn Spring Organic Farm, created this dreamy recipe. I found Renana's instructions so evocative, that I've included them verbatim.

AUBERGINE DREAM BURGERS

Renana (RJ) Fisher, Redwing Organic Farm and Robin Tunnicliffe, Llewellyn Spring Organic Farm
Makes 6 servings.

1 MEDIUM-LARGE EGGPLANT
⅔ C OLIVE OIL
2 TBSP BALSAMIC VINEGAR
1 TBSP DIJON MUSTARD
1 HEAPING TSP OF YOUR FAVOURITE WILDFLOWER HONEY
2 LARGE CLOVES GARLIC, MINCED
DASH OF SALT
DASH OF TAMARI
DASH OF YOUR FAVOURITE RED WINE
SEVERAL SLICES BLUE CHEESE

"Go to the Moss Street Market with your basket. Select the glossiest, most curvaceous eggplant from a farmer with a mysterious smile. Next, find a farmer with a sparkle in her eye and choose her rosiest, firmest garlic. Then find the honey seller with a knowing countenance and choose the jar that calls to your soul. An hour before your guests arrive, pour yourself a glass of wine and set out a marinating dish wide enough to fit six half-inch rounds of eggplant. Whisk the oil, balsamic vinegar, Dijon mustard, minced garlic, honey, salt and Tamari. Slice the eggplant across the width into half-inch rounds, place them in the marinade and set aside. Turn

them over every 10 minutes or so when you come to the kitchen to refresh your wine. After half an hour or so, transfer them to a roasting pan and cook for 30 minutes. Use the remaining marinade to dress your lovely organic salad greens, which no fine dinner party is without. After half an hour or when the eggplant is nicely grilled, remove from oven and top with a thin slice of blue cheese. Serve with your favourite burger toppings, fresh warmed buns, the tossed salad greens and wine."

SINGLE HILL FARM

4455 Leefield Road
Victoria V9C 3Y2
Tel: 478-4503
Natural
Vegetables, fruit, free-range eggs
Owner: Terry Sterling

Vegetable box program June to October, farm pick-up or delivery. Stall at Sooke Country Market and Metchosin Farmers' Market.

Terry Sterling has farmed for 15 years, and, like many growers with small market gardens, he has chosen to grow organically, but not seek certification. He feels that "Natural" is "a misleading word, as it suggests that organically grown is inferior to Certified Organic. Terry feels, that "in some cases, organically grown is a superior product, depending on how it was grown and how fresh it is."

I think one of the most appealing aspects of shopping at the farmers' markets is getting to know the growers, and coming to understand their positions on organic growing and marketing.

THERAH VALLEY FARM

Site 48, C21
Galiano Island V0N 1P0
Tel: (250) 539-2127
Fax: (250) 539-2757
moores_therah@gulfnet.sd64.bc.ca
Certified Organic
Vegetables
Owner: Therah Village Development Ltd.

Not open to the public. Produce sold at the Galiano Market.

Therah is an inspiring, sustainable community based on a 160-acre property on Galiano Island. Fifty acres is allocated to residential use where ten people live year-round, and the remainder is held co-operatively by 28 shareholders, many of whom stay on weekends or in summer. There is forested land, a lake and 25 acres of certified organic orchards and gardens. Members have established private family garden plots, both to feed themselves and for cash crops.

Barbara Moore loves the sense of community at Therah Valley Farm. She shares a commitment to holistic forest practices and consensus decision making with fellow residents, and believes that "growing organic food is a way to take responsibility for the quality of our food, to know where it comes from, and to take practical action to protect agricultural land now and into the future."

VEGETAL PÂTÉ

Rachelle Guay via Barbara Moore, Therah Valley Farm
Makes enough to fill 9 sandwiches.

¾ C WHOLE WHEAT FLOUR
½ C GROUND SUNFLOWER SEEDS
2 TBSP LEMON JUICE
⅓ C SAFFLOWER OR SUNFLOWER OIL
1 CRUSHED GARLIC CLOVE (OR MORE, TO TASTE)
⅔ C NUTRITIONAL YEAST
1 GRATED CARROT
2 GRATED ONIONS
1 GRATED CELERY STICK
1 GRATED POTATO
4 TBSP TAMARI
1 TSP DRIED BASIL
½ TSP DRIED THYME
¼ TSP DRIED SAGE
1 C HOT WATER (OR LESS)

Preheat oven to 350°F. In a large bowl, mix all the ingredients together. Spread the mixture in a 9" square casserole dish, so that it is about 1½" thick. Bake for 45 minutes to 1 hour. Let cool and remove from pan. Serve warm with a nice spicy relish, or cold as a sandwich filling.

Barbara's note: "I vary the amounts of veggies a little and personally don't use celery, so you can adapt to your own taste. I seem to

make this recipe more in the winter, using a combination of dried and fresh herbs — dried basil and oregano or marjoram, and fresh thyme and sage as it is usually still fine even in January."

TWO WINGS FARM

4768 William Head Road
Victoria V9C 3Y7
Tel: 478-3794
twowings@islandnet.com
Certified Organic
Salad greens, heirloom tomatoes, fruits, vegetables and organic seeds
Owners: Bernie and Marti Martin-Wood

Not open to public. Stalls at Metchosin Farmers' Market and Moss Street Market. Supplies Café Brio.

The dream of owning a farm came true in 1986 for former BC Tel employee Bernie Martin-Wood and his wife Marti. They had always been great gardeners, and concerned about what they fed their children. The answer was a three-acre farm in Metchosin with arable soil and views over the Juan de Fuca Strait.

Bernie had grown up on his family's dairy farm in Chilliwack and today keeps a few dairy goats, as well as laying hens. The rest of their property is given over to organic vegetables, and his highly prized heirloom tomatoes.

The Martin-Woods "saw what was going on around us, and naturally chose organics." Says Bernie, "the people who are at the forefront [of the organic movement] are environmentalists who can see that growing conventionally is very destructive to the environment." He feels it's not just about what we grow, but how we treat the earth.

PASTA WITH ROASTED VEGETABLES
Marti Martin-Wood, Two Wings Farm
Makes 4-6 servings.

TOMATOES	
ASSORTED VEGETABLES (GARLIC, ONIONS, PEPPERS, CARROTS, SUMMER SQUASH AND "WHATEVER ELSE IS ON HAND")	
OLIVE OIL	ROSEMARY AND THYME, FRESH OR DRIED
SALT	BALSAMIC VINEGAR
GRATED PARMESAN	3 C DRIED PASTA (PENNE OR RIGATONI)

FARM FRESH VEGETABLES AND HERBS

Preheat oven to 350°F. Cut the tomatoes and assorted vegetables into large chunks, and place in a single layer on a baking sheet. Drizzle with olive oil, sprinkle with salt and scatter with the herbs. Roast in oven for about 1 hour. Turn off the heat, remove the vegetables and drizzle with a little balsamic vinegar. Return the vegetables to the oven to keep warm. In a large pot, cook the pasta until *al dente*. Mix the cooked pasta with the roasted vegetables, and serve sprinkled with the Parmesan.

UMI NAMI FARM

961 Matheson Lake Road
Victoria V9C 4G9
Tel/Fax: 391-0763
Certified Organic
Oriental and Western vegetables
Owners: Yoshiko Unno and Tsutomu Suganami

Open by appointment only. Produce included in a Western Communities' box program; stall at Moss Street Market and Metchosin Country Market.

I first met Yoshiko and Tsutomu in the long line-up for succulent ostrich samples at Feast of Fields, so we had lots of time to chat. Like most farmers on a rare day off, they seemed to be enjoying the freedom.

The couple's seven-acre farm, Umi Nami, means "sea wave." It's an ocean away from Japan, but Yoshiko and Tsutomu are keeping their heritage alive. They produce a large variety of Oriental vegetables, herbs and fruits in their greenhouse including jinglebell peppers, shiso (an herb), okra, Japanese eggplant, daikon, bitter melon, Oriental green onions and Chinese cabbage, most of which are grown in the greenhouse. On the Western front, practising crop rotation and crop mixing, they grow potatoes, Granny Smith apples, beets, cabbage, broccoli, brussel sprouts and strawberries. There is also a small-scale brown-box program, catering to a dozen local families (winter box is $15; summer $15-20).

Umi Nami Farm reflects Yoshiko's simple philosophy: "We like to eat healthy food and we like people to eat good things."

DAIKON AND TOFU STIR-FRY

Yoshiko Unno, Umi Nami Farm
Makes 4 servings.

½ DAIKON
1 CARROT
PREPARED DAIKON GREENS*
1 CONTAINER FIRM TOFU
1 TBSP OIL
SOY SAUCE
SALT
COOKED RICE, TO SERVE

*Prepare daikon greens: cut below the neck, put the greens into boiling water for about 1 minute; rinse in cold water, then squeeze the water out of the greens and chop them into small bits (about ½" each).

Cut the carrot into julienne strips. Heat the oil, and add the prepared daikon and carrot. Once the vegetables become soft, add some salt, to taste. Add the tofu, chopping it into small pieces with your spatula as you add it. Add the chopped daikon greens and soy sauce to taste, and serve with rice.

Yoshiko's note: "The daikon is milder at the top (including greens) and hotter as you eat towards the tip. So the top parts are good for boiling and stir-frying, and the bottom is nice for salad."

VALHALLA FARM HERBS N' THINGS

3693 Gibbins Road
Duncan V9L 6E7
Tel: (250) 748-1741
www.valhallaherbs.com
valherb@cow-net.com
Natural
Fresh culinary herbs in season, herb plants, dried herbal blends, teas and herbal preserves
Owners: Pat and Henri Andersen

Open April to October, Saturday and Sunday, 10:00 am to 3:00 pm. Stalls at New Duncan Farmers' Market and James Bay Community Market

A former chef, Henri Andersen first started growing the herbs that he couldn't buy in Victoria (we all remember those days!). When the Andersens outgrew their Victoria garden, they moved to larger pastures. Their 12-acre property in the warm Cowichan Valley includes pastures, a deciduous hill covered with wildflowers, a creek and pond. About a quarter of the property is in cultivation. The Andersens share their idyllic setting with resident old Scottish sheep, South American Aracana chickens, and Sir George Trinkemale, a llama and the sheep's invincible bodyguard. The area's Roosevelt elk pass through regularly and snack on a few Valhalla apples en route to the Cowichan River.

The property's pièce de resistance is a large display garden, which the Andersens painstakingly carved out in front of their 1903 farmhouse. Carefully designed footpaths allow visitors to view herbs in their natural growing conditions, some in shade and others thriving in the sun. A charming respite is the homemade twig gazebo in the centre of the garden, where one can sit in summer and be lulled by the fragrance of rose and honeysuckle.

Pat feels strongly that "on Valhalla, we have a responsibility to sell an organically superior product to our customers. We work at achieving this by constantly enriching our soil, refusing to use herbicides or pesticides and protecting the environment of the farm's wildlife by leaving large areas of untouched forest."

CHICKEN WITH HERB AND MUSHROOM SAUCE

Henri Andersen, Valhalla Farm Herbs n' Things
Makes 4 servings.

1 CHICKEN, 3-5 LB, CUT INTO PIECES
¼ C WHITE WINE
¼ C FLOUR
1 TBSP HERBES DE PROVENCE*
2 TSP OLIVE OIL

Sauce

½ C ONION, FINELY CHOPPED
2 C MUSHROOMS, SLICED
¼ C MIXED RED AND GREEN PEPPERS, FINELY CHOPPED
2 TBSP BUTTER
½ C MILK
2 TBSP FLOUR (USE ANY LEFT FROM COATING THE CHICKEN)

Garnish

CHOPPED PARSLEY

* Pat suggests making your own Herbes de Provence by combining 4 tbsp thyme, 2 tbsp marjoram, 1 tbsp rosemary, 1 tbsp summer savory, 2 tsp lavender flowers and 1 tsp fennel seeds. Store in a cool, dark place and use as needed.

Preheat oven to 350°F. Combine the flour with the Herbes de Provence, and coat the chicken with this mixture. Heat the olive oil in a frying pan, and brown the chicken on both sides. Place chicken in a baking dish and finish cooking in the oven. Deglaze the frying pan with the wine, and save it in a cup. Heat the butter in the frying pan, add the onion, mushrooms and peppers and cook over moderate heat until tender. Add the flour, then the milk, and stir sauce until thickened. More milk or chicken stock can be added to thin the sauce if it is too thick. Place the cooked chicken on a serving plate, cover with the sauce, and garnish with chopped parsley.

VANCOUVER ISLAND ORGANIC FARMS

1552 Burnside Road West
Victoria V9E 2E2
Tel: 479-2454
suki@pacificcoast.net
Certified Organic
Vegetables including lettuce, beans, zucchini, beets, salad mix and a variety of potted herbs
Owners: Jon and Suki Allard

Currently not open to the public. Produce available at Capers Community Market, Lifestyle Markets, Banana Belt Fine Foods and through box programs such as Share Organics and Saanich Organics.

This is a family-run five-acre fully certified organic farm. Jon Allard feels that "organic farming allows us to contribute to a healthy, sustainable way of life for today and tomorrow. One of our objectives is to produce food in a way that protects and enhances the environment in which we live, while providing a safe, healthy and nutritious range of high quality produce. We see the future as 'organic' and are committed to developing a farming system based on these ideals."

Jon says the farm's location, just 15 minutes from downtown Victoria, is in the ideal position for "providing customers with fresh produce. Crops are picked, boxed and then delivered within hours of harvesting."

WAVE HILL FARM

340 Bridgeman Road
Salt Spring Island V8K 1W7
Tel/Fax: (250) 653-4121
Certified Organic
Strawberries, raspberries, blueberries, cascade berries, figs, apples, salad mix and specialty vegetables such as banana and purple potatoes; lamb, chicken and pork, cut flowers and eggs
Owners: Mark Whitear and Rosalie Beach

Not open to the public. Meat and poultry by special order — "please call ahead." Stall at Market-in-the-Park. Supplier of fruits to Hastings House, and herbs and flowers to Salt Spring Island Cheese Company.

Ten years ago, Mark Whitear and Rosalie Beach were living in a small English village next to a big field. The field produced wheat, barley and potatoes under a steady stream of chemical sprays, and it didn't take them long to decide to move. Says Mark, "Ironically, I felt it would be less toxic to live in London!"

They moved instead to Salt Spring Island, where Rosalie's family had held a 500-acre property for over 40 years. The land is mostly treed, and Mark practises natural selection forestry on 140 acres (he supplies the island with lumber, large timbers, firewood and split-cedar rails). There is a lovely heritage orchard with 100-year-old trees bearing Wolf River, King of Tompkins Country, Baldwin, Wadhurst Pippins, Gravenstein, Mann, Wolf River and Fallow Water varieties. And on 2½ acres, the couple has created a prolific organic market garden.

Mark says they have always grown organically because "it's the only way to grow things. Food has to be healthy and sustainable, and this fits with our own lifestyle and choices for what we eat." He holds the same philosophy for his forestry operation: "I wouldn't want to use wood from a clearcut — everything has to be managed and sustainable."

CASCADE BERRY BAKE

Rosalie Beach, Wave Hill Farm
Makes 8 servings.

¼ C BUTTER
¾ C SUGAR*
1 LARGE EGG

1 c WHOLE WHEAT PASTRY FLOUR
1 TSP BAKING POWDER
¼ TSP SALT
1½ c FRESH OR FROZEN CASCADE BERRIES**
½ c SUGAR*

* Rosalie recommends natural cane juice Sucanat sugar

** cascade berries are a cross between a wild trailing blackberry or western dewberry and a loganberry. They have just the right flavour for this recipe, but you may substitute strawberries, blackberries or blueberries.

Preheat oven to 350°F. In a mixing bowl, cream together the butter and ¾ cup sugar until smooth. Beat in the egg until the mixture is thick and lemon coloured. In another bowl, sift together the flour, baking powder and salt. Add the flour mixture to the creamed mixture and stir until the ingredients are well combined. Turn the batter into a buttered 9" x 12" ovenproof dish and spread evenly. Top the batter with the cascade berries and sprinkle with the ½ cup sugar. Bake for 30 minutes until browned at the edges and pulling away from the sides of the dish. Serve warm, topped with whipped cream or ice cream.

WINDY HILL FARM

7170 Maber Road
Saanichton V8M 1S9
Tel: 652-2777
Natural
Strawberries, raspberries, tayberries, boysenberries, loganberries (also currently testing some new berries including blueberries, lingonberries and black currants)
Owners: Stephen and Jacki Eng and Family

Open June to August, Monday to Saturday, variable hours — "please call ahead." U-pick customers should bring own containers. Limited quantities of frozen berries available out of season.

Stephen Eng says that although the farm is not certified organic, "We do everything possible to minimize the use of sprays on our fruit. We use sustainable agricultural practices which are based on good economic and environmental parameters." Some of the Engs' sustainable methods: rotate fields to keep the soil viable and reduce the carry-over of

soil-borne plant diseases (regular u-pick strawberry customers notice that the crop has moved to a new location every year); use cover crops to build up the organic matter of the soil; use biological controls to control insect pests so they do not have to use sprays; and use insect predators to control aphids and two-spotted spider mites.

TASTE OF THE ISLAND

Every summer on the August long weekend, Debbie and Derek Scott of Oldfield Orchards, 6286 Oldfield Road, Victoria, host the outdoor smorgasbord of the year. Taste of the Island gives some 60 food growers and producers the chance to showcase their wares, and the public can sample everything from emu meat to pesto. Derek says they established the event to raise awareness of the local food and beverage industry, and encourage everyone to "buy from your neighbours." A dollar from each admission is donated to local food banks. For information on attending and/or exhibiting, call Derek at 652-1579.

Organic-Gardening Projects

Some of the most inspiring organic-gardening projects are just quietly going about their business in the community.

I was delighted when horticultural consultant Jackie Robson invited me to the Colwood Garden Project. It's part of the Western Communities Organic Garden Project, an educational program dedicated to growing food for the community. Sponsored by Capital Families and the Pilgrim United Church, it gives people dealing with personal social issues the opportunity to do something satisfying for themselves and others. Project Coordinator Kelly Greenwell says there have been 40-50 people in the program in the last four years, some of whom went on to help establish a similar gardening project in Sooke.

Contact: Jackie Robson, 361-9446

LIFECYCLES
527 Michigan Street
Victoria   V8V 1S1
Tel: 383-5800
Fax: 386-3449
www.coastnet.com/lifecycles
lifecycles@coastnet.com

This is a non-profit organization dedicated to "a world that recognizes our relationship with food as key to maintaining a healthy planet." Its ambitious and highly successful programs include the Common Harvest box program, as well as:

SHARING BACKYARDS
Links people who want to garden but have no space with people who have land to spare.

COMMUNITY GARDENS
LifeCycles created the "Our Backyard" community garden on View Street, and offers resources for community groups who want to establish allotment gardens.

GROWING SCHOOLS
LifeCycles helps schools, daycares, camps and group homes create gardens with children. It can assist teachers with the planning and creation of the garden, and offer a full range of workshops and activities for the children.

DEMONSTRATION SITES
LifeCycles has restored a degraded piece of land at Holland Road and Blue Ridge Avenue, named "The Hive" after the bees who are vital to the pollination and growth of plants. The Hive serves as a demonstration organic-growing site. Visitors are welcome to learn about food growing, water conservation, pest control, soil building and garden design. Tours, workshops and training sessions are available at the site. There is another prolific garden at Menzies and Michigan streets in James Bay.

Chapter Two: Home Delivery

GETTING FRESH RIGHT ON YOUR DOORSTEP

"Find the shortest, simplest way between the earth, the hands and the mouth." (Lanza del Vasto)

When I was growing up in Victoria, it was uncommon to have produce delivered. Today, many busy and health-conscious people find that organic home delivery has become a necessity. Opening the weekly box of fresh fruit and veggies can be all the inspiration one needs to start cooking.

One executive couple I know credits home delivery with "redesigning our whole eating pattern. Instead of relying on the turgid task of going to supermarkets, our healthy diet is predetermined. We love 'Mr. Vegetable'!" (Their "Mr. Vegetable" is actually Fresh Piks Organics, but there are lots to choose from.)

Many farms offer their own locally based box programs including ALM Organic Farm, Eisenhawer Organic Produce, Umi Nami Farm and Kildara Farm.

COMMON HARVEST

527 Michigan Street
Victoria V8V 1S1
Tel: 383-5800
Fax: 386-3449
www.coastnet.com/lifecycles
lifecycles@coastnet.com
Certified Organic, Transitional and Natural
Operator: LifeCyles Project Society
Coordinator: Tara Lindsay

Full share member: $440 includes a box of produce every week for 22 weeks (June through October), weekly newsletter, invitations to the participating farms, LifeCycles events and a year-end Common Harvest celebration. Half share member: $220 includes a box of produce every second week for 22 weeks (11 boxes), bi-weekly newsletters, invitations to the farms, LifeCycle events and year-end celebration.

Bicycle delivery available to James Bay, Fairfield, Fernwood and downtown Victoria for $2.50 per box, or customer picks up in James Bay.

Common Harvest is a community-supported agriculture (CSA) endeavour run through Lifecycles, which "helps the community have a closer connection with their food and the people that grow it," says program coordinator Tara Lindsay. The program is run by young people, who also receive valuable training in business management and farming. The produce is provided by four local growers including Corner Farm, Llewellyn Farm, Froghill Farm and Kyla Neufeld's farm.

ROASTED VEGGIE SALAD
Corner Farm, Common Harvest
Makes 6 servings.

> 3 C SALAD MIX OR MIXED GREENS
> 1-2 TOMATOES, CUT INTO EIGHTHS
> ½ CUCUMBER, SLICED
> 6 C ASSORTED VEGETABLES (BEETS, TURNIPS, SQUASH, ONIONS, CARROTS, YAMS, ETC.)
> 2 TBSP OLIVE OIL
> 1-2 CLOVES GARLIC, MINCED
> SALT, FRESHLY GROUND BLACK PEPPER AND BASIL, TO TASTE

Combine the salad greens, tomatoes, and cucumber slices and set aside.

Preheat oven to 375°F. In a separate bowl, toss together the assorted vegetables with the olive oil, garlic and seasonings. Place on a baking sheet in a single layer and bake for 45 minutes or until golden, stirring the vegetables every 15 minutes. Remove the vegetables from oven and let cool slightly. Mix with the salad greens mixture. Dress with olive oil and balsamic vinegar or your favourite dressing.

FRESH PIKS ORGANICS
#3-956 Devonshire Road
Victoria V9A 4T8
Tel: 383-7969
Fax: 383-7959
www.freshpiks.com
mail@freshpiks.com
Certified Organic
Owner: Brent Hammond
Full box: $35.00, Small box: $25.00. Customized boxes and dry goods available.

Deliveries three to four days/week by vehicle or bicycle, or customer can pick up. New customers welcome.

Fresh Piks Organics is a local company that delivers fresh, organic produce right to your door. Says Brent Hammond, "We provide our customers with the finest quality produce and obtain it as close to home as possible. In the summer, most of our produce is BC grown with local as our first choice. In the winter, we buy from warmer climates in addition to as much BC produce as possible."

What began four years ago with 50 deliveries once a week has rapidly expanded to many hundreds of boxes delivered several times a week. "Our goal is to encourage the consumption of organic produce to better the health of people and the environment." says Hammond.

LINGUINI PASTA WITH CREAMY CASHEW AND MUSHROOM SAUCE

Brent Hammond, Fresh Piks Organics
Makes 6 servings.

SEA SALT
1 454-G PACKAGE LINGUINI
1-2 TBSP OLIVE OIL
1 C CARROTS, CUBED
1 C ONIONS, DICED SMALL
1 VEGETABLE BOUILLON CUBE
⅓ C HOT WATER
2 C PLAIN SOY MILK
1 C CASHEWS
1-2 TBSP OLIVE OIL
1 PINT OYSTER MUSHROOMS, SLICED
1 HEAVY PINCH SAFFRON (OPTIONAL)
SEA SALT AND BLACK PEPPER TO TASTE

Place a large pot full of water over high heat and bring to a boil. Add 1 tsp sea salt and the linguini noodles. Stir well and cook until pasta reaches desired tenderness. Strain, rinse and allow it to drain. Heat 1-2 tbsp olive oil in a medium sauce pan, and sauté the carrots and onions over medium high heat for 8-10 minutes until they are softening and the onions are browning nicely. Stir often as they cook to ensure even browning and to prevent sticking. Dissolve the bouillon cube in the hot water . Add the soy milk and set aside. In a blender or food processor, purée the dry, raw cashews until they have a fine, mealy consistency (2-3 minutes). Pour the soy/bouillon mixture into a blender with the cashews and purée for 30 seconds.

HOME DELIVERY

Turn the vegetable mixture down to medium heat, pour the bouillon liquid into the saucepan and stir briskly as the mixture thickens and bubbles. Turn heat to low and keep the sauce warm. Heat 1-2 tbsp olive oil in a medium sauté pan over medium heat. Add the mushrooms and sauté for 6-8 minutes, stirring often. Once the mushrooms are evenly browned, add them to the cashew sauce, stir well, and bring to a simmer. Taste and add seasonings to suit personal preference. Remove sauce from heat and serve hot, ladled over the fresh steaming pasta.

Brent's note: "The ground cashews will continue to soak up liquid, thus further thickening the sauce. If the sauce becomes too thick, add ¼ cup or more of soy milk and stir well. This dish is very yummy served with Caesar salad and focaccia with olive oil-balsamic vinaigrette for dipping."

POTATO LEEK PASTRY POCKETS

Brent Hammond, Fresh Piks Organics
Makes 4 servings.

Filling

3 c POTATOES, CUT INTO 1" CUBES
3 TBSP MISO, LIGHT COLOURED
3 TBSP SUNFLOWER OIL
1 TBSP STONEGROUND MUSTARD
2 TSP DRIED DILL
1 c LEEKS, SLICED THIN

Pockets

1½ c KAMUT FLOUR
1 TSP SEA SALT
2 TBSP APPLE CIDER VINEGAR
¾ c COLD WATER
½ c NON-HYDROGENATED MARGARINE OR COCONUT BUTTER*

* Brent uses Omega Nutrition's cold-pressed, organic, raw, non-hydrogenated coconut butter

Preheat oven to 375°F. Steam the potato cubes until tender. In the meantime, whisk the miso, oil, mustard and dill together to form a paste. Once the potatoes are cooked, place in a mixing bowl with the leeks and gently fold in the miso mixture. Combine the kamut flour and sea salt. Stir the vinegar into the cold water and set aside. Use a pastry cutter or two butter knives to cut the margarine into the flour mixture. Break up the bigger pieces of margarine, working the dough

as little as possible. When the dough has an even, mealy consistency, pour ½ cup of the water and vinegar over the top and lightly knead. Turn 3 or 4 times until well mixed. Add a little more of the water and vinegar mixture as needed, to create a firm ball of dough. Turn the dough ball out onto a well-floured countertop, and cut into four equal portions. Roll out one portion into a ¼" thick pastry round. Place ¼ of the potato mixture onto the pastry round, just off centre. Use fingertips and a little water to wet the edge all the way around, then fold the pastry over filling and seal edges. Repeat this process with the other three pastry portions and place each finished popover onto a lined baking sheet. Bake for 22-25 minutes until the popovers are golden. Serve with salsa, chutney, or raita.

SAANICH ORGANICS

P.O. Box 21
Brentwood Bay V8M 1R3
Tel: 652-8499
Certified Organic
Owners: Tina Fraser and Rebecca Jehn
One standard box feeds 2 people for a week — price on inquiry.

Deliveries by van on Tuesdays.

Tina Fraser, Rebecca Jehn, Renana (RJ) Fisher, Robin Tunnicliffe and Sarah Jane Smith are the dynamic women behind Saanich Organics. Rebecca says their venture is based on bringing "seasonal regional eating" to the local community. "I feel good about the quality, high nutrient value, and freshness of the produce we offer," she says.

For eight years now, the women have met once a week at one of their farms to pool their produce and make up boxes for 50 to 60 households. Rebecca delivers all the boxes in her van. When there is crop failure, that particular item is purchased from another South Island Organic Producers' Association (SIOPA) grower.

SHARE ORGANICS

1885 St. Ann Street
Victoria V8R 5V9
Tel: 595-6729
Fax: 595-6721
www.shareorganics.bc.ca
susan@shareorganics.bc.ca

Certified Organic and Transitional
Owner: Susan Tychie
Small box: $25.00, large box: $35.00

Deliveries Tuesday and Wednesday between 10:00 am and 6:00 pm, by vehicle or bicycle. New customers welcome.

Share Organics is a family-owned business that insists on local produce in season. Susan Tychie says, "Often the demand outstrips the supply, and so we have been encouraging local production by buying Transitional produce under the IOPA umbrella. To fill the gap and for variety, we next choose BC produce and products within our bio-region. In the off season, we buy from the US and Mexico."

Weekly offerings are posted on the website, and customers can make any changes they want. In addition, they can add on from the extensive list of dry goods and other organic products including fresh eggs and bread from local sources.

"Share Organics is committed to providing our community with a convenient way of receiving reasonably priced, high-quality organic produce and to supporting and promoting local growers in sustainable agriculture."

EGGPLANT LASAGNE
Susan Tychie, Share Organics
Makes 8-10 servings.

2 MEDIUM EGGPLANTS
1 TBSP OLIVE OIL
32 OZ PASTA SAUCE (YOUR OWN OR PURCHASED)
1½ C RICOTTA CHEESE
¼ C GRATED PARMESAN
½ C CHOPPED PARSLEY
1 BUNCH KALE OR CHARD
2 C GRATED MOZZARELLA CHEESE
1 LARGE EGG

Preheat oven to 350°F. Slice eggplants horizontally into ¼" rounds. Brush both sides of eggplant slices with olive oil. Place on an ungreased cookie sheet and brown under the broiler. Turn and brown other side. Mix together the ricotta, Parmesan, parsley and egg. Wash and chop the kale or chard. Layer in a 9" by 12" casserole dish or lasagne pan as follows: ⅓ pasta sauce, ⅓ eggplant slices, the cheese-egg mixture, ⅓ eggplant slices, ⅓ pasta sauce, chard or kale, 1 cup mozzarella, ⅓ eggplant, ⅓ pasta sauce. Cover and bake for 45 minutes. Uncover and top with remaining mozzarella. Continue to

bake, uncovered, for 15 minutes. Let the eggplant lasagne sit for 10 minutes before serving.

Susan's note: "This recipe uses eggplant instead of noodles. You may want to try substituting eggplant for noodles in your own lasagne recipe. I make this recipe in two bread pans — one using eggplant for adults and the other with noodles for the kids! In that case, I only use one medium eggplant."

SIMPLY ORGANICS INC.

2826 Austin Avenue
Victoria V9A 2K7
Tel/Fax: 382-3624, 382-0623
organic@islandnet.com
Certified Organic
Owner: Kim White
Custom ordering, free delivery.

Deliveries Wednesday, Thursday and Friday between 5:30 and 8:30 pm, by vehicle or customer picks up if out of delivery area. New customers welcome.

A home-based family-owned and -operated business, providing "personal service with heart," Simply Organics offers custom food baskets. You choose your own order or have one customized to your needs. All produce is local and BC certified organic; they also have certified organic groceries including dairy, eggs, meats, tofu, breads and bulk food.

"We support certified organic farming, producers of healthy soil, water, air, flora and fauna. We condone organic farming that is also deeply rooted in respect for the animals and other organisms involved in food production. Our only additives are care and responsibility."

SMOKED TOFU SUSHI

Kim White, Simply Organics Inc.
Makes 4 servings.

3-4 c sushi rice, pre-cooked and cooled*
4-6 tbsp Japanese rice vinegar*
1 package nori seaweed wrappers**
mayonnaise and honey Dijon mustard

2 CARROTS, PEELED AND GRATED
1 SMALL CUCUMBER, PEELED, SEEDED, SLICED INTO LONG THIN STRIPS
½ BAG BABY SPINACH, PRE-COOKED (STEAMED) AND COOLED
1 PACKAGE SMOKED TOFU***, SLICED INTO LONG THIN STRIPS
1 RIPE AVOCADO, CUT INTO THIN STRIPS
GOMASHIO****

* Cook the sushi rice as directed on the package, or 1 cup rice to 2 cups water. The rice should be fine and sticky, but not too mushy. Let it cool, then slowly fold in the rice vinegar to taste, and set aside.

** Kim prefers Sushi Nori seaweed wrappers which are available in Victoria's Chinatown

*** Kim uses Soya Nova smoked tofu, available from Simply Organics

**** gomashio is a seasoning composed of sea salt and toasted sesame seeds. Kim uses Val's Gomasio, available from Simply Organics

Prepare to roll up the sushi:

Lay one sheet of nori seaweed lengthwise onto a sushi mat, bamboo mat or piece of heavy wax paper.

Evenly and thinly spread a small portion of the rice across the seaweed. Dip your finger into a bowl of water, to avoid sticking to the rice.

Spread a thin coat of mayonnaise and honey mustard onto the rice layer.

Lay sparingly a variety of the prepared vegetables lengthwise on the seaweed end closest to you. Lay a thin layer of tofu with the vegetable strips.

Be careful not to have too many items in the roll!

Roll the sushi:

Roll the mat, seaweed, rice and filling.

Use a forward motion to pull the mat loose from the seaweed roll as you tightly squeeze the wrapper until you have completed a tube shape. This should hold tightly, as the sticky rice helps keep it together.

Wrap roll in wax paper, set aside, and continue wrapping more rolls.

Using a very sharp knife, cut each roll into approximately 5-6 pieces. Wipe the knife frequently to ease the cutting process.

To serve, dip one cut side of each piece of sushi into the gomashio. Arrange attractively on a plate with a side dish of tamari or soy sauce.

Chapter Three: Pick of the Shops

WHERE TO BUY ORGANIC PRODUCE. WHERE TO GET FRESH

"A few years back the government advised us to peel carrots because of the potentially harmful residues of chemicals which had been used in their cultivation. This is enough to make me feel that the real truth must be very much worse." (Nigella Lawson, *How to Eat*, Chatto & Windus, 1998)

"Organic certification is the customer's guarantee that foods are grown and handled according to strict standards, and grown without the use of synthetic fertilizers, pesticides, hormones or antibiotics." (Lynne Neufeld, Capers Community Market)

"By the year 2010, organics will take over the supermarkets." (Alex Campbell Jr., Vice President of Fresh Operations, Thrifty Foods)

Originally it was the chemicals, the contaminated groundwater, the strawberries with fish genes, the foods from America with GRAS (Generally Recognized As Safe) additives, and scares like mad-cow disease that sent me scurrying to the farmers' markets and organic grocers, but I have to admit it's taste and quality that keep me going back for more.

I choose not to feed my family sprayed produce, or bone meal-fed chickens, nor will I drink coffee from conventionally grown beans, or wine whose vines were sown using pesticides and herbicides. Granted, none of us needs the philosophy lecture to determine that the taste of organic foods is superior. If you haven't already done so, taste, compare and make your own choices.

TEN REASONS TO EAT ORGANIC*

The best reason for buying organic food is simply that it tastes extremely good but, undoubtedly, there are also sound health reasons for doing so.

It has been shown in some studies to have more vitamins and trace elements than conventionally grown food and, of course, it will not have been treated with any noxious chemicals.

It is safe, nutritious, unadulterated food. It does not use artificial chemicals, pesticides or fertilizers.

It is environmentally friendly.

It is produced without genetically modified organisms (GMOs).

It places great emphasis on animal welfare.

It is produced without the routine use of antibiotics and growth-promoting drugs.

It reduces dependence on non-renewable resources.

There has not been a case of BSE in any herd which has been in full organic management since before 1985.

It relies on a modern and scientific understanding of ecology and soil science, while also depending on traditional methods of crop rotation to ensure fertility and weed and pest control.

* from Britain's organic farming institution, the Soil Association, via the Certified Organic Associations of British Columbia (COABC).

BANANA BELT FINE FOODS

2579 Cadboro Bay Road
Victoria V8R 5J1
Tel: 592-1115
Fax: 592-2127
Certified Organic, Transitional and Natural
Full-service grocery store
Owner: Paul Large

Open daily, 8:00 am to 8:00 pm.

One-stop gourmet organic shopping found its neighbourhood when Banana Belt Fine Foods moved in next door to the venerable Slater's Meats. Now Oak Bay and Uplands shoppers can pick up their organic meat, then pop through the archway to buy almost everything else. Paul Large, son of a well-known local grocery family, thought he would be catering exclusively to a niche market when he opened his specialty store, but "as the demand for organics grows, the niche is becoming the norm — and that's been great for business."

Paul insists that "quality always comes first in our store." Banana Belt carries approximately 80% organic produce, much of which is harvested locally. Particularly in the summer months, small farmers come around with "the most beautiful organic lettuces and other produce to tantalize our customers. We have people who shop here daily, couples who come in together and plan dinner from what's fresh that day." Paul, and employees

Rob Bada and Jamie Wilkinson, love it when someone finds "that perfect purple cauliflower" or any other unusual ingredient for a special meal.

In addition to fruit and vegetables, the store carries organic cheese and milk products, fresh daily bread from Wild Fire Bakery, Salt Spring Island Roasting Company and Creekmore coffees, Denman Island Chocolate, Feys & Hobbs delectables, and even the famed (but not organic) Dean and Deluca spices and coffees. Daily specials are posted on the giant chalkboard outside.

Want a real Victoria secret? Check the *Times Colonist* for Banana Belt's annual "One Day Sale," an incredible opportunity to buy practically at cost while enjoying samples from their suppliers. It's worth the line-up!

RONNIE'S RAGOUT

Ronald Ward (a favourite customer), Banana Belt Fine Foods
Makes 8-10 servings.

3 TBSP OLIVE OIL
3 CLOVES GARLIC, PEELED AND SMASHED
3 MEDIUM YELLOW ONIONS, COARSELY CHOPPED
3 SMALL LEEKS, WHITE PARTS ONLY, THINLY SLICED
3 LARGE CARROTS, CUT INTO ½" PIECES
12 RED-SKINNED NUGGET POTATOES, EACH 1½" OR SMALLER, CIRCLE OF
  SKIN PEELED OFF MIDDLE
3 MEDIUM PARSNIPS, SLICED ON DIAGONAL, ½" THICK PIECES
1½ C CANNED CRUSHED TOMATOES
3 C VEGETABLE STOCK (CAN USE CHICKEN STOCK)
1 BOUQUET GARNI (THYME, ITALIAN PARSLEY AND BAY LEAF TIED TOGETHER)
2 LB BUTTERNUT SQUASH, PEELED AND CUT INTO BITE-SIZED CUBES
3 MEDIUM TURNIPS, CUT INTO ½" CUBES
1 TSP SPANISH PAPRIKA (HUNGARIAN IS TOO HOT FOR THIS RECIPE)
1 TSP CAYENNE PEPPER
SALT AND PEPPER
1 SMALL FENNEL BULB, SLICED INTO 2" LONG STRIPS
1 MEDIUM RED BELL PEPPER, SEEDED, CUT INTO SMALL TRIANGLES

Heat the olive oil in a large Dutch oven. Over medium heat, sweat the garlic, onion and leeks, cooking until they release their moisture. Cover pan, and let the vegetables steam themselves. Stir from time to time, and add pinches of salt and pepper halfway through the cooking. Add the carrots, nugget potatoes, parsnips, crushed tomatoes and ½ cup of the vegetable stock. Simmer for 15 minutes. Add the remaining stock, bring to a boil and then reduce to simmer. Add the bouquet garni. Add the squash, turnips, spices, salt and pepper

to taste, and cook, covered, for 20 minutes. Add the fennel and red pepper and simmer for 2 more minutes. Check and correct seasoning. Serve over rice, garnished with a sprig of thyme.

CAPERS COMMUNITY MARKET

#109-3995 Quadra Street
Victoria V8X 1J8
Tel: 727-9888
Fax: 7279832
www.wildoats.com/capers
vicofcmgr@wildoats.com
Certified Organic and Transitional
Full-service grocery store
Manager: Nancy Barber

Open daily, Monday to Saturday, 9:00 am to 9:00 pm, Sunday, 10:00 am to 7:00 pm.

Stores like Capers have given Victoria hope for an organic future! You won't find an "organic produce section" here. As Nancy Barber says, "We *only* carry organic produce. We never buy conventional. Sometimes we may have to purchase transitional but only when organic is not available."

Natural Living Consultant Lynne Neufeld describes Capers' buying strategy: "We carry the full range of organic fruits and vegetables that is available. We support local growers first. If local produce is not available, we buy from Vancouver. When we can't get a product that is BC grown, we have to go with California organic produce." Lynne gives fascinating tours of the store — just call for an appointment.

Capers also offers a complete line of other organic grocery items including eggs, cheese, chicken, grains, nuts, pasta sauces, and many gourmet items such as vinegar and olive oil. The on-site bakery labels all items with their ingredients, and there is a wide range of store-brand organic products on offer.

The deli always offers lunch, which can be eaten in the store at window tables or taken out. You'll find wraps, sandwiches, vegetarian patties, and soup that customers consistently rave about. I am often pleasantly surprised by the "Customer Appreciation Days," when cashiers take 10% off everyone's grocery bill.

THAI GREENS

Susan Smith, Chef, Capers Community Market
Makes 4 servings.

> 1 BUNCH KALE, ROUGHLY CHOPPED
> 1 BUNCH CHARD (RED, IF YOU LIKE), ROUGHLY CHOPPED
> 1 BUNCH BROCCOLI, CUT INTO FLORETS AND JULIENNED STALKS
> ⅓ C FRESH LIME JUICE
> ⅓ C KETSOP MANIS*
> 2 CLOVES GARLIC, MINCED
> ½-1 TSP SAMBEL OLEK**
> ¼ C CILANTRO, CHOPPED
> PEANUTS FOR GARNISH

*sweet soy sauce, available at Asian markets and many groceries

**red pepper sauce, available at Asian markets and many groceries

Steam the greens individually and lightly. Mix together and set aside. Combine the lime juice, ketsop manis, garlic and sambel olek. Drizzle dressing over the greens. Garnish with the cilantro and peanuts.

RAINBOW EGG FOO YONG

Lynne Neufeld, Natural Living Consultant, Capers Community Market
Makes 2-4 servings.

> 2 GREEN ONIONS, MINCED (INCLUDE BOTH WHITE AND GREEN PARTS)
> ¼ C BELL PEPPERS (GREEN, RED AND YELLOW OR OTHER COMBINATION), DICED
> ¼ C CELERY, DICED
> 1½ C ZUCCHINI, GRATED
> 2 C MUNG BEAN SPROUTS, CHOPPED
> 4 EGGS
> ¼ C RICE FLOUR
> 1 TBSP BRAGGS LIQUID AMINOS*
> ¼ TSP GINGER ROOT, GRATED OR ½ TSP GINGER POWDER
> 1 CLOVE GARLIC, PRESSED OR ¼ TSP GARLIC POWDER

*a seasoning made of soybeans and purified water

Combine all veggies in a large mixing bowl, and set aside. In another bowl, beat the eggs lightly with a whisk and then whisk in the rice flour, liquid aminos, ginger and garlic. Pour mixture over the veggies and mix well. Drop the egg foo yong by ¼ cup measures into a hot oiled (or non-stick) skillet. Brown on both sides and serve immediately.

COLWOOD HOUSE OF NUTRITION
#6-310 Goldstream Avenue
Colwood V9B 2W3
Tel: 478-3244
Fax: 478-3057
biosupply@biosupply.com
Certified Organic, Transitional (T2+) only rarely
Full-service grocery store
Owners: Elfriede Juergensen and Peter Juergensen

Open Monday to Thursday, and Saturday, 9:30 am to 6:00 pm, Friday, 9:30 am to 7:00 pm, Sunday, 11:00 am to 5:00 pm. Closed Christmas Day, Boxing Day, New Year's Day and Easter.

Elfriede Juergensen is in many ways the matriarch of the organic movement in these parts. In the early 1980s, she and her son Peter were making weekly visits to Wild West Organic Distributors in Vancouver to load up on healthy produce for their store. Today, the elder Juergensens enjoy travelling, while Peter continues the family tradition of seeking out high quality organic foods.

Over a cup of the store's choice Frontier coffee, he told me that his own interest in organics "has to do mostly with the user of the products. I think people have to be more aware of what goes into food. The growing techniques used by organic farmers ensure nutrients are put back into the soil, and this means we are ingesting a higher value food product."

Peter's customers are mainly women with families, seniors, and first-time mothers who want the best nutrition for their babies. "It often starts with that firstborn child eating organically, and now we can look back to two or three generations of many families as customers."

The store is immaculate and chock-full of dry goods, produce, dairy, breads, vitamins and health and beauty products. You'll find Olympic and Nancy's yogurts, Shinmeido Miso, Big Root Apple Juice, Eden Organics, Healthy Times Baby Food, Tinyáda pastas, unsweetened German baking chocolate and Wild Fire baked goods, to name only a few items. In-store demonstrations give customers ideas about food preparation, and Peter's staff are extremely knowledgeable.

PETER'S MUESLI

Peter Juergensen, Colwood House of Nutrition
Makes 1 serving.

- 1 TBSP CHOPPED TOASTED ALMONDS
- 1 TBSP FRESH GROUND FLAX SEEDS
- ⅓ C FRESH RAW ROLLED OATS
- 1 TBSP RAW HULLED SUNFLOWER SEEDS
- ¼ C FRESH FRUIT
- 3 TBSP HOME-MADE YOGURT
- ⅛ C APPLE JUICE

Place the almonds, flax seeds, oats, and sunflower seeds into your cereal bowl and mix together. Add the apple juice (or fruit juice of choice) and stir. Top with the fresh fruit and yogurt and serve.

Peter's note: "Toast the almonds in the oven on a cookie sheet at 350°F until they begin to brown (5-10 minutes). Cool and chop to desired size. I often make enough for a couple of weeks at a time. I also roll my oats and flax fresh in my flaker to optimize the nutrient value. This breakfast will keep you and the family going until lunch, and provides you with an excellent range of nutrients and fibre. Enjoy!"

THE COMMUNITY FARM STORE

3633 Glenora Road
Duncan V9L 6S3
Tel: (250) 748-6227
Fax: (250) 748-6292
nickwell@island.net
Certified Organic, Transitional and Natural
Full-service grocery store
Owners: Susan Minette and Susan Wells

Open year-round Monday to Friday, 9:00 am to 5:00 pm, Saturday, 10:00 am to 4:00 pm. Also open on Sundays in July, August and September, 10:00 am to 4:00 pm. Represented at the New Duncan Farmers' Market on Saturdays.

Nestled amongst huge fir trees in the heart of Duncan's historic farming community is a delightful country store with a 1920s false front and front porch, where co-owner Susan Wells says, "You'd expect to see rocking chairs." Instead, there is an inviting display of produce that takes

me back to earlier times when everyone farmed organically, but without needing the label. From its beginning as an outlet for one family's organic crops, The Community Farm Store has expanded to encompass a full range of organic and high quality local products.

Susan Minette was the store's baker when the opportunity for ownership came up. She and partner Susan Wells pooled their resources and became owners in 1999. They whole-heartedly "support the production and distribution of products that contribute towards healthy children, families, individuals, communities and global economies. Our store offers products that are produced with minimum impact on the environment, that are traded fairly and whenever possible, that are produced locally."

Susan Minette, a past administrator of IOPA, grew up on Galiano Island where she worked in the family's grocery store. Baking has always been a passion and today she produces the daily fresh breads and treats made with organic ingredients. Her artisan breads include challah, and I can honestly say I drive to the store expressly for her cinnamon buns. Susan Wells, who managed the famed Duncan Farmers' Market for three years, chose vegetarianism as a teenager to be "part of a solution." As a hands-on organic grocer, she feels she is continuing that commitment.

The store runs an active produce box program which supplies 50 to 100 local families, depending on the season. There are five choices in the program, with delivery or pick-up available Wednesday through Sunday. Many customers take advantage of bulk purchasing, ordering 25- and 50-pound sacks of flour or cases of their favourite organic pasta sauces at substantial savings.

GINGER SCONES
Susan Minette, The Community Farm Store
Makes about 36 scones, depending on size of cutter.

6 C WHOLE WHEAT FLOUR
½ C SUGAR*
4 TBSP NON-ALUM BAKING POWDER
PINCH OF SALT
1¼ C ALL-VEGETABLE SHORTENING
2 C MILK
1 C CRYSTALIZED GINGER, CUT INTO SMALL PIECES
1 TBSP POWDERED GINGER

*Susan recommends natural cane juice Sucanut sugar

Preheat oven to 375°F. Mix dry ingredients in a large bowl. Cut in shortening until it resembles small peas. Add milk all at once, and gently stir until mixture holds together. Pat out dough on a floured board until ¾" thick, then cut scones into desired shape. Bake for 10 to 15 minutes or until done.

Susan's note: "The Community Farm Store is famous for these scones!"

DEMITASSE BAKERY STORE

2164 McNeill Avenue
Victoria V8S 2Y3
Tel: 598-6668
Fax: 598-3134
demitasses@hotmail.com
Certified Organic
Small full-service grocery and bakery
Owners: Rob and Catherine Rogers

Open daily, 7:30 am to 7:30 pm. Closed Christmas Day, Boxing Day, New Year's Day and Easter.

The Demitasse Bakery Store brought a welcome sea change to the neighbourhood. Sure, it is still our corner store, and we often drop in just for milk, but now we can also load up on gourmet organic dried pasta, coffee and teas, free-range chickens, olive oils, condiments, cheese from the Salt Spring Island Cheese Company and others, Denman Island Chocolate, Holy Humous and Golda's Finest Foods. The daily coffee on tap is often organic, and it always goes well with a fresh-baked croissant, eaten with neighbours on benches in front of the store.

Rob and Catherine Rogers have brought the same flair and belief in the quality of fresh, natural ingredients that they were known for downtown at The Demitasse Coffee Bar. Says Rob, "We go for almost anything organic we can get our hands on. It tastes better, and our customers tend to care about what they eat."

There is also a great selection of specialty plants and organic seedlings for sale in season.

ROASTED VEGETABLE AND CHÈVRE TERRINE
Mary Patterson, Demitasse Bakery Store
Makes 8-10 servings.

2½ LB EGGPLANT
3 LB ZUCCHINI
4 LB YELLOW AND RED PEPPERS
4 TBSP BASIL PESTO
4½ OZ GOOD QUALITY CHÈVRE
SALT AND FRESHLY GROUND BLACK PEPPER
OLIVE OIL
2 9" x 5" LOAF PANS
2 28-OZ TIN CANS (UNOPENED)
PLASTIC WRAP

Thinly slice the eggplant and zucchini. Lightly salt the eggplant and let it rest in a colander to drain (about 30 minutes). Toss the zucchini slices with a little salt and olive oil. Lay them in a single layer on a baking tray. Split the peppers in half, and remove the seeds. Treat the peppers and drained eggplant like the zucchini, placing the vegetables in single layers on baking sheets. Roast all the vegetables for 20 to 30 minutes at 350°F. Transfer the roasted peppers to a bowl, cover tightly with plastic wrap and sweat for 30 minutes. Remove the skins. Line one loaf pan with plastic wrap, letting it flow over the sides. Begin laying the peppers, 1 tablespoon pesto, eggplant, zucchini, another tablespoon pesto, the sliced chèvre, zucchini, pesto, eggplant, pesto, and finally, the remaining peppers. Place another piece of plastic wrap loosely over the pan, top with the other loaf pan in upright postion, and weigh the whole down with the two tins. Place in the fridge overnight, then un-mold the terrine, and slice to serve.

LIFESTYLE MARKETS
#180-2950 Douglas Street
Victoria V8T 4N4
Tel: 384-3388
Fax: 384-3050
www.lifestylemarkets.com
lifestylemarkets@home.com
Certified Organic, Transitional and Natural
Full-service grocery store
General Manager: Carmine Sparanese
Store Manager: Ryan Mackey

Open daily, Monday to Saturday, 9:00 am to 8:00 pm; Sundays and Holidays, 10:00 am to 6:00 pm.
Also opening new stores soon at 3838 Cadboro Bay Road and 343 Cook Street.

Ryan Mackey says the market is "committed to offering the finest selection of certified organic products on our shelves," and that "the finest natural or conventional alternatives are sought out only when organics are not available."

Lifestyle Markets is one of the city's few full-service organic foods stores, where everything from vitamins to produce to dairy is on offer. Mackey says "Customers come for the organic produce and good prices, but they also enjoy the whole experience of shopping here." Company philosophy holds that exchanging information is vital to give people a reason to eat naturally. Many free publications and a well-used bulletin board in the deli/restaurant keep shoppers abreast of the latest food and wellness news.

Chef Paul Patterson presents lively and informative bi-weekly cooking demonstrations in the store. These are great opportunities to learn from a true advocate of whole foods cooking. The following recipe is from Paul's recently released cookbook, *Chef Paul's Whole Foods Cookbook* (Ensure Visions Consulting, 2000).

BUTTERNUT SQUASH PEPPERCORN PENNE
Chef Paul, Lifestyle Markets
Makes 2-4 servings.

1 C BUTTERNUT SQUASH, CUT INTO ½" CUBES
1 TBSP MINCED GARLIC
1 TBSP OLIVE OIL
1 RED ONION, JULIENNED
1 RED BELL PEPPER, CUT INTO ¼" PIECES
1 Portobello MUSHROOM, CUT INTO ½" CUBES
½ PACKAGE KAMUT PENNE*, COOKED AL DENTE
2 TSP GREEN PEPPERCORNS*
8 OLIVES, SLICED
1 PACKAGE BASIL LEAVES, CHOPPED JUST BEFORE USING
½ CAN PASTA SAUCE*

*Chef Paul recommends Artisan Acres kamut penne, Madagascar green peppercorns and Simply Natural pasta sauce for this recipe

Heat the olive oil in a medium skillet over medium high heat. Sauté the garlic and cubes of butternut squash until tender. Be very

gentle with the squash to avoid it turning to mush. Add the red pepper, red onion, olives and peppercorns to the skillet, and sauté until the onion becomes translucent. Add the mushrooms and sauté for about 2-3 minutes, then fold in the basil. Add the desired amount of pasta sauce, and reduce heat to simmer. Fold in the cooked penne, serve, and enjoy!

LIFESTYLE SELECT
Unit C - 9769 5th Street
Sidney V8L 2X1
Tel: 656-2326
Fax: 656-2881
Certified Organic and Natural
Full-service grocery store
Owner: Vita Ventures
Manager: Alanna Sparanese

Open Monday to Saturday, 9:00 am to 5:30 pm, Sunday, 12:00 noon to 5:00 pm. Closed statutory holidays.

Catering to Sidney and the Peninsula, Lifestyle Select carries a wide variety of organics, with large selections of wheat-free and sugar-free items. You'll find cookies, herbal teas, coffee substitutes, jams, nut butters, crackers, alternative cereals, soy and oat milks, a bulk section with mostly organic products, and healthy snacks without refined sugars or dairy. There's a good choice of organic baking supplies, oils, bulk herbs, soups, rice and alternative pastas in all shapes and sizes, dairy products, dried fruits, a wide section of beverages, and a select choice of organic fruits and vegetables.

Alanna Sparanese says, "We believe that in today's world, it is essential to consume nothing but the best. This means whole foods, uncontaminated and in their natural state. In supporting this, we carry organic and natural foods for healthy living and a healthy you — inside and out!"

BEET HEAVEN
Alanna Sparanese, Lifestyle Select
Makes 4-6 servings.

2-4 TBSP BUTTER
1 C FINELY CHOPPED ONIONS
4 TART APPLES, CHOPPED

6 MEDIUM BEETS
1-2 TBSP HONEY (TO TASTE)
¼ C RASPBERRY VINEGAR
2 TBSP GRATED FRESH GINGER
1 TSP SALT (OR TO TASTE)

Place the beets in a saucepan, cover with water and boil until tender, approximately 40 minutes. When cool enough to handle, discard the skin and chop the beets. Set aside. Melt the butter in a large skillet, and sauté onions until caramelized, about 15 minutes. Add the apples, honey, raspberry vinegar and ginger, and simmer uncovered 15-20 minutes, until tender. Transfer the apple mixture to a food processor, add the beets, and process until smooth. Return the purée to a saucepan and reheat.

Alanna's note: "Serve hot with holiday meals, or cold as a delicious dip for carrot sticks."

MARKET ON YATES

903 Yates Street
Victoria V8V 3M4
Tel: 381-6000
Certified Organic
Full-service grocery store
Manager: Darryl Hein

Open daily, 7:00 am to 10:00 pm. Closed Christmas Day and New Year's Day.

This is a dream market for urban dwellers, with everything from a juice bar and take-out foods, to a full-service florist and butcher. Organics are nicely integrated on the shelves, with lots of what you're looking for, including specialty products from Earth's Best baby food, Just Pick't orange juice, La Boulange breads, Dayspring tofu, Santa Cruz juices to Salt Spring Roasting Company coffees and Amy's frozen pizza.

MATTICK'S FARM MARKET

5325 Cordova Bay Road
Victoria V8Y 2L3
Tel: 658-4554
Fax: 658-3734
matfarmmkt@home.com

PICK OF THE SHOPS

Organic, Transitional and Natural
Full-service grocery store
Owners: Randy Andres and Bob Fowles

Open daily, 7:00 am to 7:00 pm. Closed Christmas Day, Boxing Day and
New Year's Day.

This is a bright, airy store that caters mainly to Cordova Bay residents, but also draws many out-of-area visitors, who simply enjoy the drive out and the many interesting shops on the former Mattick's Farm property.

Randy Andres and Bob Fowles decided to include organics from the day they opened three years ago, and customer demand has kept them on the shelves. Randy says, "Organics are a personal choice. We feel that in today's marketplace the consumer must be given the choice, whether by quality or price comparison, to initiate their first purchase towards healthy, chemical-free eating."

STUFFED PORTOBELLO MUSHROOM

Randy Andres, Mattick's Farm Market
Makes 1 serving.

1 LARGE PORTOBELLO MUSHROOM
1 GREEN ONION, THINLY SLICED
1 CLOVE GARLIC, CHOPPED FINE
1 TBSP DICED PEPPER (RED, YELLOW OR GREEN)
2 TBSP CHOPPED SAUSAGE OR SEAFOOD
¼ C DRY BREADCRUMBS
⅓ C GRATED AGED CHEDDAR
1 EGG

Preheat oven to 350°F. Brush off any dirt from the Portobello mushroom, remove stem and chop it into small pieces. Mix the chopped mushroom stem, green onion, garlic, peppers, chopped sausage or seafood, and the breadcrumbs. Add ½ cup of the grated Cheddar, and mix well. Add the egg and combine until a ball is formed. Stuff the mushroom cap (there is no need to scoop it out) with the vegetable-seafood mixture, and sprinkle the remaining Cheddar on top. Bake the mushroom for 20-25 minutes or until the cheese is melted.

Randy's note: "Serve hot with a Caesar or side salad. This is a versatile recipe that can be altered many ways."

PEPPERS FOODS

3829 Cadboro Bay Road
Victoria V8N 4G1
Tel: 477-6513
www.peppersfood.net
Certified Organic
Full-service grocery store
Owner: John Davitz

Open Monday to Friday, 8:00 am to 9:00 pm, Saturday and Sunday,
8:00 am to 7:30 pm. Closed Christmas Day, Boxing Day and New Year's Day.

In the last 23 years, John Davitz has given Cadboro Bay and Ten Mile
Point residents a practically perfect grocery store. In the last four
years, he has slowly but surely integrated organics into every department. "It's what our customers want, and I think it's healthy," says John,
who chooses organics himself as much as possible.

A tour of the shelves with John is thrilling for those of us always looking for the organic alternative. You will find Santa Cruz and Knudsen
juices, Shari Ann's beans and soups, So Good and Soycup soy milks,
Stonyfield yogurt, Organic Meadow cheeses, Pacific and Imagine broths,
Salt Spring Island Cheese Company goat cheese, Pavich orange juice,
Kicking Horse, Seattle's Best and Salt Spring Island Roasting Company
coffees, Happy Planet juices and even organic snack food like Little Bear
cheese puffs and QuePasa taco chips. There's a Nature Clean alternative
for every conventional cleaning product in stock, as well as Seventh
Generation paper towels and toilet paper. Lyndie's organic breads from
Shawnigan Lake are hard to resist.

John's meat department carries frozen organic chicken, and they can
order other free-range meats including game, on 24-hours notice. When
it came to sharing a recipe, John graciously deferred to Eileen Bender, his
deli manager, who is personally "making the switch" to organics.

CREAMY GOAT CHEESE AND ROASTED PEPPER STUFFED CHICKEN BREASTS

Eileen Bender, Peppers Foods
Makes 4 servings.

1 ROASTED SWEET RED PEPPER, PEELED, SEEDED AND CUT INTO ½" STRIPS
4 OZ GOAT CHEESE*
4 BONELESS, SKINLESS CHICKEN BREASTS (750 G)

1 TBSP OLIVE OIL
¾ C CHICKEN BROTH*
½ C DRY WHITE WINE OR CHICKEN STOCK
½ C HALF & HALF CREAM*
1 TBSP CHOPPED FRESH THYME
2 TBSP FINELY CHOPPED RED ONION
¼ TSP GROUND BLACK PEPPER
4 FRESH SPRIGS OF THYME, TO GARNISH

*Eileen uses Salt Spring Island Cheese Company goat cheese, Pacific fat-free chicken broth, and Valley Pride half & half cream

Mix together the red pepper strips and goat cheese. Divide mixture into four equal portions, and set aside. Insert a small knife horizontally into the thickest edge of each chicken breast to form pocket (try to keep the entrance to the pocket as small as possible). Carefully stuff each breast with a portion of the pepper/cheese mixture. Heat the olive oil in a large skillet over medium-high heat. Brown the chicken for about 4 minutes. Add the chicken broth and wine, and bring to a boil. Reduce heat to low, cover the skillet, and simmer for 6-7 minutes or until the chicken is cooked through. Transfer the chicken to a heated plate and cover to keep warm. Return the skillet to high heat and boil until the liquid is reduced to ¾ cup (about 5 minutes). Stir in the cream, thyme and red onion, and continue to boil for another 5 minutes or until the liquid is reduced to ½ cup. Stir in the black pepper. To serve, pour a pool of sauce on each of 4 dinner plates. Cut each stuffed chicken breast diagonally into 4 or 5 slices and arrange on top of the sauce. Finish with a sprig of fresh thyme.

Eileen's note: "For a delicious alternative, substitute sundried tomatoes for the roasted red peppers."

SEED OF LIFE NATURAL FOODS

1316 Government Street
Victoria V8W 1Y8
Tel: 382-4343
Certified Organic
Full-service grocery store
Owners: The Sharpe Family

Open Monday to Saturday, 9:00 am to 6:00 pm. Sunday, 12:00 noon to 5:00 pm.

When one of Dorothy Sharpe's young sons ordered yogurt and granola out of the blue during a trip to Port Angeles years ago, she had no idea his dietary inclinations would lead to the family's owning a health food store. Seed of Life Natural Foods, a Victoria institution that began life as a co-op in 1970, has been operated by the Sharpes for six years. Located in Victoria's true downtown, the store caters to a hearteningly diverse urban crowd.

Produce comes from local certified organic farmers or from the lower mainland, with fresh fruits such as oranges, bananas and mangoes shipped from the United States. The extensive bulk-foods section includes organic whole grains, flour, legumes, seed, nuts and dried fruit, and the store also supplies organic cheese, milk, eggs and other grocery items.

Dorothy Sharpe says her family's philosophy is "to provide our customers with the best quality organic foods possible, at the best prices. We also assist our customers with solving their individual dietary requirements."

THRIFTY FOODS

6649 Butler Crescent
Saanichton V8M 1Z7
Tel: customer service line 544-1234
www.thriftyfoods.com
info@thriftyfoods.com
Certified Organic section, Transitional produce only rarely
Full-service grocery stores (17 stores throughout Victoria, Colwood, Central Saanich, Sidney, Mill Bay and Salt Spring Island).
Owner: All stores are locally owned and operated.
Vice President of Fresh Operations: Alex Campbell, Jr.

Open early morning to late evening – check individual stores for exact hours.

Thrifty Foods has made a big effort to integrate organic foods such as milk and cheeses, processed and packaged dry foods, canned and frozen foods, snack bars and beverages in their stores. The organic produce sections are always fresh, and staff assigned to these areas are consistently knowledgeable and helpful. The stores' buyers visit local and California farms several times each year to check that organic standards are being met.

Surprisingly, when Thrifty Foods originally introduced organic produce in 1989, it received a poor reception from consumers, with more

produce thrown out than sold. Organics were re-introduced in 1992, and the rest is a happy history of steadily increased demand. Today, organics account for 10% of produce sales.

Alex Campbell, Jr., feels strongly that "if the consumer had been given a choice in the 1940s and 50s, production would probably not have gone to chemical based as did happen. Consumers have the right to choose organic for their own health and the health of the planet."

The Thrify Foods website is useful to check out the week's in-store specials and pick up some great recipes.

FRUIT SALAD WITH HONEY AND MINT DRESSING

Chef Yauki Leung, Thrifty Foods, Admirals Walk Store
Makes 8-10 servings.

Salad

¼ SMALL WATERMELON, SEEDED AND DICED
½ MEDIUM CANTALOUPE, SEEDED AND DICED
½ MEDIUM HONEYDEW, SEEDED AND DICED
½ MEDIUM PINEAPPLE, CORED AND DICED
2 C RED SEEDLESS GRAPES
8 MEDIUM KIWIS, PEELED AND DICED
2 LARGE ORANGES, PEELED AND CUBED

Dressing

¼ C FRESH ORANGE JUICE
½ C FRESH LIME JUICE
⅓ C HONEY
¼ C CHOPPED FRESH MINT
DASH OF CINNAMON

Put all cut fruits in a large bowl. In a medium size bowl, combine orange juice, lime juice, honey, mint and cinnamon. Whisk to blend. Add the dressing to the fruits. Toss to combine well, then refrigerate for 1 hour.

Yauki's note: "Serve with finger sandwiches and assorted cheeses."

WEST COAST NATURAL FOODS

6716 West Coast Road
Sooke V0S 1N0
Tel: 642-4011
Organic, Transitional and Natural

Full-service grocery store (limited produce).
Owner: Lorraine Hoy

Open Monday to Saturday, 9:30 am to 5:30 pm. Closed Christmas Day, Boxing Day Sale and New Year's Day.

Lorraine Hoy says she runs a mostly organic food store because she is "trying to get it right," and watching her in action, there is no doubt she is succeeding. In only a few minutes, she helped a teenage girl sort out a natural skin-care regimen, took an order for milk thistle tea to clear up a customer's liver problems, sold a couple of burly gentlemen some tea tree oil, and found organic tomato juice for someone else.

She has been a proponent of healthy, natural eating for a long time, describing herself as having done "the whole Mother Earth thing – spinning, farming and feeding my family with produce, eggs, and meat from one-and-a-half acres." Lorraine feels her interest in organics is simply an extension of the life she has always led.

Her store is well stocked with organic products such as Choice and Yogi teas, Greene's Farm tinned vegetables, Eden beans, Prairie Harvest dried pasta, Golden Temple granola, L'Ancêtre cheeses, Tugwell Honey, EnviroKidz cereals, Soyganic Baked Tofu and Denman Island Chocolate. There is a big choice of staples like rice, beans and flours, and an impressive vitamin and body-care section including lines like Burt's, Weleda and Druide.

LORRAINE'S GRANOLA

Lorraine Hoy, West Coast Natural Foods
Makes 30 ½-cup servings.

8 C LARGE-FLAKE ROLLED OATS	1 C SUNFLOWER SEEDS
SPRINKLE OF SALT	1 C COCONUT
1 C WHOLE ALMONDS	½ C SESAME SEEDS
1 C PUMPKIN SEEDS	½ C FLAX SEEDS
1 C PECAN HALVES	1 C SAFFLO OR CANOLA OIL
1 C WHOLE CASHEWS	1 C HONEY OR MAPLE SYRUP

Preheat oven to 300°F. In a large roasting pan, combine all dry ingredients with your hands. Drizzle with the oil, then the honey, without mixing. Place pan in oven. When the honey begins to melt, stir it into the oat mixture. Continue to bake, stirring frequently, for about 1 hour, or until everything is golden. Turn the oven off, open the oven door, and let the granola cool before removing the pan (the granola will become nice and crunchy). Serve ½ cup of the granola with yogurt, fresh fruit, and a drizzle of flax oil.

Lorraine's note: "Granola makes a great gift. I gave some to my doctor, and he loved it! I also take it when I travel for healthy snacking."

AMARANTH FOOD FOR THOUGHT

B132 (across from the Cinecenta box office)
Student Union Building
University of Victoria
Victoria V8P 5C2
Tel: 472-4386
Certified Organic
Full-service co-op grocery store
Manager: Beatrice Emmanuel

Open Monday to Friday, 10:00 am to 3:00 pm.

For as long as I've been a UVic student (a long time, don't ask!) Amaranth has provided students, faculty and the general public with an opportunity to buy local, organically grown or distributed food at wholesale prices. Operating from a small space, it has a big impact on the health and well being of the university population. You don't have to be a scholar to shop there.

You can shop for items in the store, or order from the vast catalogue of goods. Handy order forms can be filled out and dropped through the shop door even in off hours. You'll find grains, seeds and cooking supplies, cereals and granola, soy and rice milk, dried and frozen fruit and vegetables, herbal tinctures, fresh baked breads (from Wild Fire Bakery), eggs, environmentally friendly cleaning products and natural hygiene products. Each time you order, you can choose to donate 50¢ (or more) to the university's food bank.

PENINSULA CO-OP

2132 Keating Cross Road
Saanichton V8M 2A6
Tel: 652-1188
Fax: 652-5769

customerservice@peninsulaco-op.com
Certified Organic
Full-service co-op grocery store
General Manager: Pat Fafard

Open Monday to Saturday, 8:30 am to 9:00 pm, Sundays and holidays, 9:00 am to 6:00 pm.

The Peninsula Co-op offers an interesting alternative to conventional grocery shopping. The store is member-owned, but, as Pat Fafard says, "You don't have to be a member to shop with us."

It's a large, well-laid-out store, and as the co-op philosophy advocates disseminating information, there is an impressive "site map" to help you find everything. Although mainly conventional, the store carries organic produce, dairy items, and packaged goods such as pasta, canned vegetables, coffee, cereal and baby food. Products are supplied by a number of organic wholesalers and, "Wherever possible, we purchase products locally from the Saanich Peninsula farmers."

As in many conventional grocery stores, the organics have come about largely by customer request. Pat explains: "Many of our members expressed an interest in purchasing organic items, so we developed an organic product mix for them to purchase."

WHAT IS A CO-OP?

Co-ops give members the benefits of partial ownership where they shop for groceries. Co-ops are locally owned and controlled by their members. Anyone can buy shares in a co-op (usually for $10 to $30 per share plus a small administrative fee) and the benefits include an annual return on investment in cash and/or shares.

Co-ops are guided by seven internationally recognized principles:

Voluntary and open membership;

Democratic member control;

Member economic participation;

Autonomy and independence;

Education, training and information;

Co-operation among co-operatives; and

Concerns for community.

PICK OF THE SHOPS | CO-OPS

For more information, visit a local co-op or contact:
Ministry of Finance and Corporate Relations
Societies and Co-operatives Unit
P.O. Box 9431, Station Prov. Gov.
Victoria V8W 9V3
Tel: 356-8673

Chapter Four: The Staff of Life

AND OTHER FOODS WE CAN'T LIVE WITHOUT

"Why go organic? There's not much choice not to!" (Cliff Lier, Wild Fire Bakery)

MERRIDALE HOUSE SOURDOUGH BREADS

1236 Merridale Road
RR #1
Cobble Hill V0R 1L0
Tel/Fax: (250) 743-8225
dugan@virtualbc.org
Certified Organic
Bread
Owner: Judith Daniel

Not open to the public, but Judith will bake to order or you can make an appointment to pick up fresh frozen loaves. Merridale Breads are available in the Cowichan Valley at Red Apple, Vitality Health Products, Mercia's Enterprise, Lynn's Vitamin Gallery and Practical Magic. Bread is sold at the Frayne Centre Market from May through September.

I first picked up a loaf of Judith's kamut bread at the Red Apple in Mill Bay, and was delighted when she offered that particular recipe for this book. She describes bread-making as "a thread that's always run through my life," and, having "always wanted to make a difference, this is my way of making a difference."

Judith has been health conscious since the 1950s and ran a health food store in Brentwood Bay for many years. Bread baking now keeps her in touch with the industry she loves, and she enjoys introducing people to the delicious taste of organic bread.

Her bakery is a small, commercial, home-based operation, where she often produces 100 loaves a week. The grains are stone-ground in a

Schnitzer Mill, and she prepares her sourdough culture from organic flour and water. For a one-person business that started in January 2000, the range of breads is impressive: spelt, kamut, 100% rye (pumpernickel), whole wheat, multigrain and organic white. All are baked as standard loaves or French style, and many already have cult followings: Cheese and Sun-dried Tomato White French, Garlic and Rosemary White French and the Christmas Braid with Fruits and Aniseed. Judith also sells a dried starter, for those not wanting to wait to try the following recipe.

"My philosophy is that true satisfaction comes from creating a product that enhances health, is life-giving and gives me a sense of continuing an ageless tradition," says Judith. "I regard also that my bread represents a live art form which awakens all our senses."

KAMUT BREAD
Judith Daniel, Merridale House Sourdough Breads
Makes 2 loaves.

    4 C SOURDOUGH CULTURE (RECIPE FOLLOWS)
    1 C WATER
    2 TSP SALT
    2 TBSP BROWN SUGAR
    ¼ C SUNFLOWER OIL
    1 C RYE FLOUR
    1 C KAMUT FLOUR
    4 C WHITE FLOUR

To make the sourdough culture, stir together and let sit for 12 weeks in a warm room:

    2 TBSP STARTER*
    3 C WHITE FLOUR
    2 C WARM WATER

Measure the sourdough culture into a large mixing bowl. Warm the water (75-85°F), and add to the culture. Mix together the salt, sugar and oil, and add to the culture.

Add the rye and kamut flours and mix well. Add the white flour, 1 cup at a time, until the mixture is too stiff to mix by hand. Turn onto a floured board, knead and add flour until the dough is smooth and satiny. Divide the dough into 2 equal pieces, form into loaves and place into greased 9" x 5" loaf pans. Cover, and let rise in a warm place (85°F) for 2 to 3 hours, until the dough rises 1"-2" above edges of the pans. Preheat oven to 350°F and bake the loaves for 50-55 minutes. Remove the loaves and cool on wire racks.

*Making Starter with Judith Daniel

"It is possible to capture your own culture simply by exposing a mixture of flour and water to the air. Combine 2 cups of good quality bread flour (I recommend starting with white flour and then transferring the culture to whichever flour is desired) and with 1½ cups of warm water in a 2 quart plastic, glass or stainless steel bowl. Stir the mixture with sufficient vigour to beat in additional air. Expose the bowl and its contents to the air, preferably outside, although it can be done inside as well. Do not cover the bowl with plastic or anything that will exclude the organisms you are attempting to collect. If insects or other critters are a potential problem, cover the bowl with a fine-mesh screen or cheesecloth. Stir the mixture vigorously at least twice every 24 hours. In 2 or 3 days, bubbles should appear on the surface as the first indication that you have been successful. Feed the culture an additional cup of flour and sufficient water to maintain the consistency, and stir it briskly again. You may need to repeat this additional feeding at 12-hour intervals for several successive days.

"When you capture a yeast that is active enough to be useful, it will form a layer of foam 1 to 2 inches deep. If it doesn't attain this level of activity in 4 to 5 days, you should probably abandon the attempt and repeat the process in a different location. There are no guarantees, and you may encounter problems with contamination by undesirable organisms, particularly in areas with air pollution. These organisms usually produce a bad odour or flavour, but are harmless. Once you have a good, bubbly culture, transfer it to one or more glass jars and refrigerate it (don't freeze it). It is now ready for use."

NATURE'S GIFTS

841 Kangaroo Road
Victoria V9C 4E2
Tel: 592-7628
Fax: 592-7641
vonweltin@yahoo.com
Certified Organic
Bread, cereals and other baked goods
Owner: Vera von Weltin

Not open to the public, but you can place an order by phone for home delivery. Nature's Gifts breads are sold at the Pandora Winter Market, James Bay Community Market, Sidney Summer Market and Metchosin Farmers' Market.

THE STAFF OF LIFE BREAD

Vera learned to bake as a "Bio-Bäcker" in her native Germany, and her bakery operation here follows the rules of the Bio-Bäckers' Association: "We promote wholefoods [sic] as nature produces it — nothing added, nothing taken away. We freshly stone-grind or flake the grains and seeds ourselves for each batch! Our most important equipment is a stone mill and flaking machine, which is the prerequisite for organic bakeries in Europe, also called 'mill-bakeries'."

Vera produces wheat-free and sugar-free baked goods such as breads (spelt, flax, 6-grain, rye and kamut), stöllen and biscotti, as well as frozen pizza dough and "Swiss style" raw cereals such as muesli. She uses mostly local or Canadian-grown certified organic ingredients, and there are no artificial additives or added fat. Vera kindly translated this recipe from the German, and it is both easy to make and delicious.

CHEESE AND STINGING NETTLE BRIOCHE
Vera von Weltin, Nature's Gifts
Makes 1 loaf.

½ TSP UNPASTEURIZED HONEY
40 GRAMS FRESH YEAST OR 2 TBSP DRY YEAST
4 EGGS
1 TBSP NETTLE MUSTARD (MIX 1 TBSP NETTLE TOPS INTO AN 8-OZ JAR OF DIJON MUSTARD — THE REMAINDER CAN BE STORED IN THE REFRIGERATOR)
½ TSP HERB SALT*
GROUND BLACK PEPPER TO TASTE
100 G BUTTER
100 G FRESHLY GROUND WHOLE SPELT FLOUR
1 MEDIUM ONION, FINELY CHOPPED
2 TBSP EXTRA VIRGIN OLIVE OIL
100 G GRUYÈRE CHEESE (OR OTHER HEARTY, STRONGLY-FLAVOURED CHEESE)
1 HANDFUL YOUNG STINGING NETTLE TOPS*
BUTTER AND FLOUR FOR THE BAKING PAN

*Vera's notes: "Herbamore Salt is recommended. Fresh nettles are best from March to May. Don't pick beside a busy street, and do take only the tops — about 20 cm off the top. When nettles are not in season, replace with Italian parsley."

Preheat oven to 425°F. Combine honey, yeast and 3 tbsp lukewarm water. Mix the eggs with the custard, and season with salt and pepper. Melt the butter, and cool slightly. Add to the eggs. Sauté the onion in the olive oil until translucent. Cut the cheese into small cubes. Wash the nettle tops in hot water (to avoid stinging!), pluck

into small pieces. In a large mixing bowl, use a wooden spoon to mix all ingredients together into a dough. Let rise in a warm place for ½ hour. Grease and flour a baking pan. Transfer the dough into the baking pan, and bake for about 30-40 minutes.

Vera's note: "Serve warm with a salad and a glass of white wine. This brioche can also be prepared ahead and frozen."

OTTAVIO ITALIAN BAKERY AND DELICATESSEN

2232 Oak Bay Avenue
Victoria V8R 1G5
Tel/Fax: 592-4080
Certified Organic, Transitional and Natural
Bread and other baked goods
Owners: Andrew Moyer and Monica Pozzolo

Open Tuesday to Saturday, 9:00 am to 5:30 pm; occasional holiday closures.

Andrew Moyer says Ottavio is "a 'gastronomia' for those who choose ingredients and finished food products that are high quality and natural," and the store pleases even the fussiest gastronome. It has certainly contributed to the civilization of Oak Bay Avenue, where one often sees a good crusty Ottavio baguette, baked using traditional techniques and non-modified ingredients, tucked under a stroller's tweedy arm. The neatly stacked breads, cookies and pastries from their own bakery, and the vast display of deli items evoke a shop in Tuscany, and that, together with the very genial staff, is what charms the shop's many appreciative customers.

Andrew points to "over 75 cheeses, both local and imported (including David Wood's fine goat cheeses), olives plain and spiced, cured meats, high quality olive oils and other Mediterranean cooking ingredients, with organic choices in most products. We make a range of sauces for pasta, homemade lasagna and tapenades, and carry local sausages and pâté. We strive to carry products made by smaller producers with fresh *real* ingredients."

This is a shop where the local customer base has responded positively to high quality, always natural, ingredients. Andrew feels strongly that "to make high quality, healthy food you need high quality, healthy ingredients. As food growers, producers and consumers, we need to act as a supportive community to nurture a safe, sustainable food supply."

THE STAFF OF LIFE BREAD

WILD FIRE BAKERY
1517 Quadra Street
Victoria V8W 2L3
Tel: 381-3473
Certified Organic
Bread and pastry
Owners: Cliff Lier and Erica Heyerman

Open Tuesday to Saturday, 7:30 am to 6:00 pm. Closed for two weeks after Christmas.

I love watching bakers in action, so when Cliff Lier asked if I minded interviewing him while he baked, I flew there like wildfire. There's something very swinging about Wild Fire Bakery. The owners and staff are all young and passionate about what they do, the location is downtown, but with that slightly "off Broadway" edge, the bakery/café is brick and wood and bright, and the music (like Devo's Greatest Hits) keeps everything very much in the groove.

A couple of years ago, an old friend persuaded Cliff to build a wood-fired brick oven at home. It produced just 12 loaves at a time, so when he and partner Erica Heyerman decided to sell their wares at the Moss Street Market, Cliff worked 30 hours straight to bake 170 loaves. Erica would sell them "in five minutes" at the market the next day, and they could already see the writing on the wall. It was time to open a bakery.

Wild Fire opened in April 1999 and it's a sell-out success every day. The artisan breads include whole spelt, white spelt, sprouted wheat, rye, whole wheat, country white and challah on Fridays. There are wheat-free options, and all breads start with a French style *levain* rising agent, which Cliff says delivers "more of a balance between acidic and lactic acids, meaning it is more easily digested." You'll find lovely mushroom shaped meringues, cookies, muffins, croissants and pannettone at Christmas.

Cliff never thought about *not* going organic because of "personal health and the health of the planet." He points out that organic baking is more difficult, as getting industrial volumes of ingredients like butter means ordering from Quebec, and everything costs more. Still, he feels that the price of organic foods are "more reflective of the real cost of real food," and knows that the more people buy, the cheaper organics will become.

Wild Fire serves organic fair trade coffee, roasted by Café Fantastico, and their window seats are great places to perch during your coffee break.

CHOCOLATE FUDGE COOKIES

Cliff Lier, Wild Fire Bakery
Makes 22 cookies.

8 OZ CHOCOLATE*
6½ OZ SUGAR
2½ OZ BUTTER
1 TSP VANILLA EXTRACT
2 LARGE EGGS
4½ OZ PASTRY FLOUR
1 OZ COCOA
1 TSP BAKING POWDER

*Cliff uses Bernard Callebaut dark chocolate

Preheat oven to 350°F. In a small saucepan or in a microwave, melt the chocolate. Set aside. In a mixing bowl, cream together the butter and sugar. Add vanilla and eggs, and mix in. Finally, add the chocolate and mix together. In another mixing bowl, sift together the pastry flour, cocoa and baking powder. Add the dry ingredients to the wet. Drop by tablespoons onto ungreased baking sheet, and bake until slightly underdone.

MOONSTRUCK ORGANIC CHEESE INC.

1306 Beddis Road
Salt Spring Island V8K 2C9
Tel: (250) 537-4987
grace@saltspring.com
Certified Organic
Cow's cheese
Owners: Susan and Julia Grace

Open May 1 to November 1, Monday to Friday, 1:00 to 4:00 pm. Moonstruck Cheese is available in Victoria at the Market on Yates, Spinnakers, Capers, Ottavio and The Wine Barrel.

THE STAFF OF LIFE

CHEESE

Originally, Susan and Julia grew vegetables which they sold at the Salt Spring Island Market. The idea to produce cheese came later, but it has become their passion. The organic farmstead cheeses from the milk of their Jersey cows includes such toothsome delights as "Blue Moon," "Blossom's Blue," "White Grace" and "Fromage Blanc." Rich in flavour and just the right size for the cheese tray, these cheeses are made from French and British recipes.

As Julia says, "We want to produce the most flavourful cheeses that we can. We believe that feeding the cows organically and treating them naturally is the way to do this. The cheese can never be better than the milk from which it came — that's why the care and feeding of our small Jersey herd is the cornerstone of our operation."

BLOSSOM'S BLUE PASTA

Julia Grace, Moonstruck Organic Cheese Inc.
Serves 4 (or 2 really hungry people!).

3 TBSP BUTTER
3 TBSP BLOSSOM'S BLUE CHEESE
1 TSP LEMON ZEST
1 TSP LEMON JUICE
1-2 C WATER FROM COOKING THE PASTA
FRESHLY GROUND BLACK PEPPER
DASH OF NUTMEG
SPRIGS OF FRESH ROSEMARY
COOKED PASTA FOR 4 PEOPLE
PARMESAN AND SOME ADDITIONAL CRUMBLED BLOSSOM'S BLUE,
IF DESIRED

In a large skillet, melt the butter gently over low heat and add the Blossom's Blue. Stir the cheese until melted. Add the lemon zest and lemon juice more or less as desired according to taste, then stir in the pasta water by the ½ cupful until the desired consistency is attained. Add the remaining ingredients to taste, and then toss the sauce over hot pasta. Sprinkle with Parmesan and more Blossom's Blue, if you like, and serve immediately.

Julia's note: "This is a light velvety sauce that goes well on shell pasta or any pasta that has lots of ridges and is not too heavy."

SALT SPRING ISLAND CHEESE
285 Reynolds Road
Salt Spring Island V8K 1Y2
Tel: (250) 653-2300
Fax: (250) 653-2308
wood@saltspring.com
Natural
Sheep and goat cheese
Owners: David and Nancy Wood
Open on Sundays of long weekends, or by appointment. Cheeses are available in Victoria at Thrifty Foods, Capers, Ottavio, Italian Bakery, Cheryl's Gourmet Pantry, Demitasse Bakery Store and Peppers Foods.

Having introduced Toronto to gourmet food through David Wood's Fine Foods in Yorkville, the Woods are now impressing west-coast chefs and home cooks alike with their artisan cheeses.

I visited during the annual Apple Festival in November. Their dream acreage includes a herd of sheep and an immaculate cheese factory, where the emphasis is on natural production. Milk from the sheep and from goats on two other farms is hand-made into cheese using traditional methods. A variety of flavours and decorative accents from lemon peel to pansies make Salt Spring Island Cheese instantly recognizable.

David says they "try to make the best quality cheese possible, at a price that is fair to everyone – milk producer, employees and consumers." He is "hoping to be able to justify the extra cost of organic feed at some time in the future."

Chocolate

DENMAN ISLAND CHOCOLATE
Site 136, C5
Denman Island V0R 1T0
Tel: (250) 335-2418
Fax: (250) 335-0112
www.denmanislandchocolate.com
info@denmanislandchocolate.com

Certified Organic
Chocolate bars and truffles
Owners: Daniel and Ruth Terry

Not open to the public. Products found throughout Victoria at natural food stores and at Sooke Harbour House, Colwood House of Nutrition, West Coast Natural Foods in Sooke, and on BC Ferries. Also served at the Governor General's residence in Ottawa.

Here's a "one bite is all it takes" story that began for me at Feast of Fields with Ruth Terry's offer of a raspberry truffle. Now I have a sixth sense for the attractive wooden display cases of Denman Island Chocolate bars, because surely "organic" takes the calories out of eating chocolate!

All Denman Island Chocolate products are certified organic and dairy-free. The chocolate bars are a specialty, made with fine Belgian chocolate, Fraser Valley hazelnuts and raspberries, fair-traded Nicaraguan coffee, and pure orange and mint essences imported from England. There are other delightful chocolate creations, too, like little toads and Father Christmases.

Ruth believes in "running an ethical business and creating the best possible product. Our goal is to convince people that eating organic may be virtuous, but it is far from boring!"

CHOCOLATE CHUNK COOKIES*

Ruth Terry, Denman Island Chocolate
*adapted from a recipe in *Recipes from an Ecological Kitchen* by Lorna J. Sass
Makes 14 large cookies.

    2 C WHOLE WHEAT PASTRY FLOUR
    ½ C ROLLED OATS
    ½ TSP SALT
    ¼ TSP BAKING SODA
    ⅔ C COARSELY CHOPPED WALNUTS OR HAZELNUTS
    1 C DARK CHOCOLATE CHUNKS
    ⅓ C LIQUID HONEY
    ½ C OIL*
    1 TSP VANILLA
    ¼ C WATER

    *Ruth uses Omega Safflower Oil

Preheat oven to 375°F. In a mixing bowl, combine the flour, oats, salt and baking soda and stir in the nuts and chocolate chunks. In

another bowl, stir together the honey, oil, vanilla and water. Stir the wet ingredients into the dry mixture until the flour is just absorbed. Using an oiled quarter cup measure, scoop 14 balls out of the mixture, placing each on an oiled cookie sheet. Flatten gently until the cookies are approximately 4" in diameter. Bake in the centre of the oven for 12-15 minutes, or until lightly browned.

Ruth's note: "Don't eat too many at once. Save some for later!"

PENINSULA ROASTING COMPANY

9514 Maryland Drive
Sidney V8L 2R6
Tel: 24-hour orders: 655-1463, administration: 655-0449
Fax: 655-0490
freshlyroasted@home.com
Certified Organic
Coffee -- fair trade, shade grown
Owner: Jan Townley

Not open to the public. Individual product deliveries on Wednesdays and Fridays. Sold at local markets in season including the Peninsula Country Market and Christmas markets such as In a Manger, Touch of Salt Spring, Last Chance Christmas Fair, Peninsula Community Association Christmas Fair. Also available for school fund-raising programs.

Opened in 1999, Peninsula Roasting Company already serves 300 customers, including 30 regular individual deliveries a week. They have an enterprising school fund-raising program underway which helps schools raise money for extra events. It's a family enterprise, with Jan's husband and father-in-law operating the roaster, and Jan marketing, serving customers and keeping the books.

They import the raw coffee beans from brokers in Vancouver and Washington, and roast to order in an environmentally friendly fluidized-bed roaster. Jan says that during this process, "Beans are roasted by clean hot air rather than the traditional method of direct flame. As a result, our

THE STAFF OF LIFE COFFEE

coffee does not taste burnt and has not accumulated volatiles during the roasting process." She sees a trend towards small batch roasting micro-roasteries, just like the micro-brewery movement, and says it makes sense because, "the more you roast, the more the quality decreases."

Coffees currently on offer include Costa Rican, Cuban Peaberry, El Salvador, Sumatra, Mexican Swiss Water Decafinated, Half-Caff Blend, Jakarta Blend and Sombrilla Blend. Says Jan, "Organic coffee not only benefits the consumer with high quality and chemical-free coffee, but also benefits the coffee farmers and workers."

Her aim is to produce a cup of coffee that gives customers a feeling of "balance, like feng shui." Ultimately, Jan says which coffee you drink "depends on your priorities — if you care about what you're putting in your body and if you're looking for great taste, you'll want to try organic."

ESPRESSO CHOCOLATE BISCOTTI

Jan Townley, Peninsula Roasting Company
Makes about 50 cookies.

2 C UNBLEACHED ALL-PURPOSE FLOUR
⅔ C GRANULATED SUGAR (PREFERABLY RAW)
1 TBSP MEDIUM GROUND FRESHLY ROASTED ORGANIC COFFEE
½ TSP BAKING POWDER
½ TSP BAKING SODA
½ TSP CINNAMON
½ C WHOLE UNBLANCHED ALMONDS
½ C SMALL CHUNKS OF DARK UNSWEETENED CHOCOLATE*
⅓ C HONEY
⅓ C HOT, STRONG COFFEE

Topping

¼ C GRANULATED SUGAR (PREFERABLY RAW)
½ TSP CINNAMON

*Jan prefers Bernard Callebaut

Preheat oven to 350°F. In a large bowl, combine the flour, sugar, ground coffee, baking powder, baking soda and cinnamon. Stir together well, and add the almonds and chocolate chunks. In a small bowl, combine the honey and hot coffee. Stir into the flour mixture until it forms stiff dough. Divide the dough in half, and shape each half into a log about 15 inches long. Place the logs at least 2 inches apart on a non-stick or parchment-paper lined baking sheet, and bake for 30 minutes, or until well risen, firm and golden. Cool logs for about 15 minutes and place on a cutting board. Cut on the diagonal

into ½" slices. On a plate, combine the sugar and cinnamon topping. Dip one side of each cookie into the cinnamon sugar. Return cookies to the baking pan, cinnamon sugar side up, and bake for 15 minutes longer, until dry and lightly coloured.

WHAT IS FAIR TRADE?

When you see the Fair Trade label on coffee, drinking chocolate, chocolate bars, orange juice, tea, honey, sugar or bananas, this is what it tells you about the production conditions and trading relations for that product:

Small scale farmers can participate in a democratic organization;

Plantation/factory workers can participate in trade union activities and have decent wages, housing and health and safety standards;

There is no forced or child labour;

Programs are in place to improve environmental sustainability;

The price charged covers the cost of production;

There is a social premium being levied to improve conditions;

An advance payment has been made to avoid small producer organizations falling into debt; and

Contracts are in place that allow long term production planning and sustainable production practices.

For more information:

Transfair Canada/Fair TradeMark

323 Chapel Street, 2nd Floor

Ottawa, Ontario K1N 7Z2

Tel: (613) 563-3351

Fax: (613) 237-5969

www.web.net/fairtrade

fairtrade@cyberus.ca

SALT SPRING ROASTING COMPANY

211 Horel Road
Salt Spring Island V8K 2A4
Tel: (250) 653-2366
Fax: (250) 653-4110

THE STAFF OF LIFE   COFFEE

www.saltspringroasting.com
coffee@saltspring.com
Certified Organic
Coffee – fair trade, shade grown
Owners: Robbyn Scott and Mickey McLeod

Salt Spring Roasting Company coffee is available at the company's two cafés on Salt Spring Island: Fulford Café and Ganges Café, and at the company's Roasting Room. In Duncan: Cavenaugh's Gallery & Cyber Café, Island Bagel, Café Rusticano, Country Grocer; in Victoria: Banana Belt Café, Market on Yates, Lifestyle Markets, Bagel Oasis, Peninsula Co-op, Peppers Foods and Country Grocer.

The Salt Spring Island Roasting Company was founded in 1996 by two coffee lovers with a strong interest in the environment. Mickey McLeod notes that, "Most of the coffee is purchased from small farms or co-ops, and we work closely with our coffee importers who regularly visit the coffee farms and co-ops to make sure the growing practices are sustainable and meet the standards we require."

GOLDA'S FINEST FOODS INC.
RR #2
Mill Bay VOR 2PO
Tel: (250) 743-3844
Fax (250) 743-8996
www.goldasfinest.com
info@goldasfinest.com
Natural
Pesto and sauces
Owner: Richard Lewin

Not open to the public. Golda's products available at over 60 food shops and restaurants from Reggie's Veggies in Duncan to the Lifestyle Markets' deli in Victoria.

Between bites of roasted eggplant at Zambri's, Richard Lewin holds court. Really, is there anyone this gentleman doesn't know? The fact is, his enthusiasm for all things — especially dahlias, literacy programs, and all things pesto — is infectious.

The Golda's story is well known, but always worth repeating, and best told by Richard himself, the "stay-at-home dad with a flair for cooking." His daughter Golda was four years old, when Dad started experimenting in the kitchen, and the rest is culinary history. Son Freeman has since joined the family operation with his Freeman's Farm and Seeds.

The basil and other produce is home-grown organically on the family's two-acre farm. Richard says there are "no chemicals in the fields or in the kitchen," and some ingredients, like the arugula, mezuna (in the hemp pesto) and garlic are certified organic. Interestingly, Richard cites kosher certification as more reliable and consistent, and says he will go for kosher certification "when cheese is kosher."

And the dahlias? Richard grows them, too, on top of the growing, harvesting, producing, packaging and exuberant marketing of the pesto.

GOLDA'S FINEST LATKES
Richard Lewin, Golda's Finest Foods Inc.
Makes about 20 latkes.

4 MED POTATOES, WASHED, SKIN ON AND COARSELY SHREDDED
2 LG CARROTS, PEELED AND COARSELY SHREDDED
4 MED PARSNIPS, COARSELY CHOPPED
1 LG ONION, COARSELY CHOPPED
¾ C ALL PURPOSE FLOUR
3 EGGS, BEATEN
SALT AND COARSELY GROUND BLACK PEPPER
1 C VEGETABLE OIL

Let the shredded potatoes sit in a colander inside a large bowl for 20 minutes. In another bowl, toss the carrots, parsnips and onion with the flour, beaten eggs, salt and pepper. Use your hands to sqeeze out any remaining liquid from the grated potatoes. Fold in the veggie mixture, and mix well. In a large skillet or paella pan, heat ¼" of vegetable oil on medium head. With your hands, shape the mixture into 3" pancakes and drop into the hot oil. Brown both sides. Set the latkes on paper towels to absorb the oil.

"Then," says Richard, "the fun begins! Try dipping your latkes in Golda's pestos: Artichoke, for a Mediterranean feast; Basil, for a night in Northern Italy; Sundried Tomato, for Southern Italy;

Cilantro, for a taste of the French Riviera; Arugula, for an art exhibit nosh; Hemp, for a retro 60s bash; and Skoogk with sour cream for Thai or Persian festivities."

Author's note: "Chanukah will never be the same again!"

DAYSPRING SOYACRAFT CORPORATION
#5-626 Esquimalt Road
Victoria V9A 3L4
Tel: 382-2144
Fax: 480-5115
Certified Organic
Soy food products including tofu, beverages, and cheese (Ridgeview brand). Also sell okara, for organic gardening and animal feed.
Owner: Paul Hsieh

Open by appointment only.

Paul Hsieh started producing tofu and soymilk from whole soy beans in 1981, "using the most traditional processing methods to ensure simple, pure and wholesome soy foods for better health and a better environment." Since then, he's made over 1.6 million pounds of tofu and 1.3 million litres of milk. His products are popular, particularly among people with dietary restrictions such as lactose intolerance.

EGGLESS TOFU SALAD
Paul Hsieh, Dayspring Soyacraft Corporation
Makes about 3 cups.

½ PKG MEDIUM FIRM TOFU*
3 TBSP APPLE CIDER VINEGAR
1½ TBSP SWEETENER OF CHOICE
1 TSP ONION POWDER
1 TSP TURMERIC

½ TSP SALT
½ TBSP GARLIC POWDER
½ PKG FIRM TOFU**
½ C CHOPPED CELERY
½ C FINELY GRATED CARROT (OPTIONAL)
½ C CHOPPED CUCUMBER (OPTIONAL)
¼ C CHOPPED ONION
¼ C CHOPPED PARSLEY

*Paul uses half of the 454 g Dayspring Medium Firm Tofu

**Paul uses half of the 454 g Dayspring Firm Tofu

In a blender or food processor, blend the medium firm tofu, vinegar, sweetener, onion powder, turmeric, salt and garlic powder until smooth. Set aside. Crumble the firm tofu into a bowl, and mix in the celery, carrot, cucumber, onion and parsley. Stir in the blended tofu mixture, and serve.

Paul's note: "This versatile salad can fill a sandwich, stuff a pita, top a bed of lettuce or stuff a tomato, or serve as a dip or spread with vegetables, chips or crackers."

FORT STREET LIQUOR STORE

1960 Foul Bay Road
Victoria V8R 5A7
Tel: 952-4220
Fax: 595-0768
www.bcliquorstores.com
larry.arnold@bcliquorstores.com
Organic (not necessarily certified) and Natural
Full-service liquor store
Owner: Government of British Columbia
Product Consultant: Larry Arnold

Open Monday to Saturday, 9:30 am to 11:00 pm. Closed statutory holidays.

THE STAFF OF LIFE

WINE

Standing in the middle of the busiest liquor store in Victoria, Larry Arnold points to a sign of the times: "Organic Wines." This small display was instituted only a year ago, but it's attracting a lot of attention.

"At first, it was the twenty-somethings who were asking for organic wines," says Larry, "but now we see more of a cross-section of people looking for healthy alternatives." I asked whether the wines are actually certified organic, and whether or not there are consistent standards. Basically, no and no. A French label says, "each year we fertilise with organic compost," and a Californian red contains "organically grown grapes." Larry says many vineyards are reluctant to certify because of cost and the lack of consistent certification standards.

The 15 or so wines on offer are either "classified as organic or they employ organic growing methods," and they include Italian of which Chianti Classico-Coltibuono, Merlot-Villa Teresa Vini Tonon, and Cabernet-Boxco del Merlo are examples, French Vin de Pays-Chapoutier La Ciboise and Comte Cathare-Château de Mont Ahuc, Chilean Chardonnay-Carmen Nativa, Bulgarian Merlot-Vinprom Haskovo, Argentinian Malbec-Humberto Canale Diego Muillo and Californian Sirah Bonterra.

ROASTED RED PEPPER AND BAKED GARLIC SOUP

Larry Arnold, Fort Street Liquor Store
Makes 4 servings.

6 RED PEPPERS
3 HEADS (BULBS) OF GARLIC
VEGETABLE STOCK
WHIPPING CREAM
OLIVE OIL
SALT AND PEPPER
FRESH ROSEMARY SPRIGS TO GARNISH

Preheat oven to 375°F. Cut the red peppers in half, remove the seeds and ribs and place cut side on a cookie sheet. Roast in oven until blackened. Sweat in a paper bag for 15 minutes, then peel off skins. Set aside. Cut tops off the garlic bulbs, and place bulbs in a small baking dish. Sprinkle with olive oil, salt and pepper and roast until the garlic is soft, approximately 20 minutes. Squeeze the garlic pulp out of skins and put in a food processor. Add the roasted peppers and purée. Gently heat the purée in a saucepan, adding vegetable stock until desired thickness is reached. Finish off with whipping cream

to taste. Serve in bowls with a dollop of crème fraiche, a grinding of black pepper, and a sprig of rosemary.

Larry's note: "Enjoy this soup with a slightly chilled red organic wine such as a cabernet (if you can find one), and excellent conversation."

MARK ANTHONY WINE MERCHANTS

2560A Sinclair Road
Victoria V8N 1B8
Tel: 721-5222
Fax: 721-5272
saanich@markanthonys.com
Certified Organic and Natural
Wines and accessories
Owner: Anthony Von Mandl
Manager: Amy De Paoli

Open year round Monday to Sunday, 10:00 am to 9:00 pm. Closed Christmas Day and New Year's Day.

Like its two counterparts in Vancouver, this very charming shop carries an assortment of organic wines including Mission Hill's Maréchal Foch from British Columbia, Chapoutier from France, and California's Bonterra (five types) and Kenwood (the single-vineyard Upper Weise zinfandel).

The store opened in 1989, and Amy De Paoli has noticed an increase in inquiries about organic wines in the last two years. Many people report that they have fewer or no headaches from drinking the organic varieties. She would "like to see more organics, but it is difficult to get certification in British Columbia."

Assistant Manager Neely Hourigan says, "It's a pleasure to sell a product that has been cared for from the vine to the bottle. One can only hope that it will become more economically viable for more vintners to pursue organic growing practices."

THE VQA* WINE SHOP AT MATTICK'S FARM

#133-5325 Cordova Bay Road
Victoria V8Y 2L3
Tel: 658-3116

Fax: 658-3117
vqashop@home.com
*Vintners Quality Alliance
Organic (not certified)
VQA wines, preserves, books and accessories
Owner: Beth Crawford
Manager: Renée Willows

Open Sunday to Friday, 10:00 am to 6:00 pm, Saturday, 10:00 am to 7:00 pm.

When The VQA Wine Shop opened three years ago, they already had organic wines on offer. Renée Willows, who remembers the property when Mr. Mattick was growing and selling produce and offering pony rides, says people aren't specifically asking for organics, but many want fewer sulphites. She naturally directs them to the Hainle Pinot Blanc or Traminer, or to the Summerhill selections: Ehrenfelser, Chardonnay, Merlot, Pinot Noir and Cabernet Franc Merlot, all made from organically grown grapes without added sulphites.

THE WINE BARREL
644 Broughton Street
Victoria V8W 1C9
Tel: 388-0606
Fax: 385-0630
www.bcwine.com/thewinebarrel
thewinebarrel@home.com
Certified Organic, Transitional and Natural
BC VQA wines and some food items including Moonstruck cheeses, and Feys & Hobbs' multigrain wafers.
Owners: Wilf Krutzmann and Carol Morgan

Open Monday to Saturday, 10:00 am to 7:00 pm, Sunday, 12:00 noon to 5:00 pm.

Wilf points out that going organic is "a financial struggle for the little vineyards," so there really are just a few in organic production. British Columbia's Hainle Vineyards is the only totally certified organic vineyard in all of Canada. Others, like Summerhill Estate Winery, have certified organic vineyards but the buildings are not yet certified. St. Hubertus has some organic vineyards, but they also buy grapes from non-certified vineyards. The good news is that many vineyards are heading towards organic conditions, even though they have not yet reached certification standards.

An increasing number of Wine Barrel customers ask for organic wine. Wilf believes that "Anything that can be done to guarantee consumers are buying a quality product can only benefit the wine industry as a whole." He thinks the answer lies in educating people on the many benefits of drinking organic wine, from personal health to great taste to environmental sustainability.

Organic Cleaning Products

Natural, toxin-free cleaning products from Seventh Generation, Nature Clean and others are available at most food shops mentioned in this chapter.

GEORGIA STRAIT ALLIANCE

195 Commercial Street
Nanaimo V9R 5G5
Toxic Smart Program Coordinator: Cathy Booler (250) 753-3459
www.georgiastrait.org
gsa@georgiastrait.org

Under the Georgia Strait Alliance's Toxic Smart Program, your organization can learn to be smart about toxic products in the home, and become knowledgeable about water conservation, energy efficiency, and proper sealing techniques. In conjunction with Environment Canada, the Alliance developed a home visit program, to sweep your house of harmful toxins and give advice on natural cleaning alternatives.

THE STAFF OF LIFE

CLEANING PRODUCTS

The following are some of their "recipes."

ALL PURPOSE CLEANER

Combine ½ cup pure soap with 1 gallon hot water OR ¼ cup baking soda or borax with 4 cups hot water. To cut grease, add ¼ cup lemon juice.

GLASS CLEANER

Add 4 tablespoons vinegar or 1 tablespoon lemon juice to a spray bottle filled with warm water. Polish away!

DRAIN CLEANER

Cover the drains with a screen to keep out debris. Use a plumber's snake or plunger to clear the drain. Pour ½ cup vinegar and ½ cup baking soda into the drain. Cover tightly for 1 minute, then flush. Next, use ½ cup salt and ½ cup baking soda and 6 cups of boiling water. Let sit several hours; then flush with water.

Chapter Five: Seasonal Markets

FRESH SEASONAL BOUNTIES FROM LOCAL GROWERS AND FOOD
PRODUCERS

SEASONAL MARKETS

"Find the honey seller with a knowing countenance and
choose the jar that calls to your soul." (Renana Fisher, Redwing
Organic Farm)

It's no wonder that farmers' markets have captured our culinary
imagination and brought new social energy to our neighbourhoods.
What greater pleasure than to buy produce picked only hours before
from the person who planted and nurtured it? I value the relationships
I've developed with growers, and give them all the credit when someone
compliments me on a particular dish. My salads are fresher and more
interesting because of the just-harvested mesclun I buy at Moss Street
Market, my stuffed, baked figs taste better when the chèvre comes
directly from its maker at the Salt Spring Market-in-the-Park, and the
honey that "called to my soul" at the Peninsula Country Market elevates
my baklava. As Chef Jason MacIsaac of Point No Point says, "The finest
food begins with the finest ingredients," and many of the finest ingredients can be found at the new celebration of farmers' markets, where
every stall is an emblem of commitment to eating well.

If you do go to market, take your thermos of tea and head out early. It's
fun to watch from afar as the growers set up their stalls. My mother and
I eye the veggies, fruit, cheese, bread and other fresh foods being
unpacked, and we've already planned our menus by the time the bell
rings, signifying that the stalls are open for business.

A couple of tips for the uninitiated: farmers' markets are part of the
solution, so please take your own shopping bags, and growers love questions, so don't be shy. If you don't recognize a vegetable on display, ask.
Growers are constantly changing the offerings on their stalls, and love to
share a new discovery. Often, they will offer samples to spark discussion.
Looking for a new ways to serve produce? Ask again! How do you think
I got all these great recipes?

Included here are the markets that offer a good choice of organic produce. Generally, local farmers' markets are open from May through
October, but dates vary, so call for exact schedules. Market information
is also listed in the daily and weekly newspapers.

CEDAR FARMERS' MARKET
On Yellow Point Road at the Crow and Gate Pub
Sundays, 10:00 am to 1:00 pm, May to October
Contact: George Benson
Tel/Fax: (250) 722-3526

Mostly organic growers including Yellow Point Orchards, Bensons' Olde Tyme Farm, Limberlost Orchard, Golden Maples Farm, Big D Emu Farm, Gabriola Gourmet Garlic and Munro Creek Farm. Homemade bread and baked goods from the Cedar Womens' Institute. Some crafts.

Cedar Farmers' Market has been going strong for over six years. Its recent move from the Cedar Community Hall to a field beside the Crow and Gate Pub has been hugely successful, as folks can now combine organic shopping with a nice pub lunch!

This is a small, friendly market with lots of choice. Some days, Juno award winner Ken Hamm drops by to play his blues guitar, and every season there's a zucchini car race for the children.

FRAYNE CENTRE MARKET
On the parking lot between The Coffee Mill and Caitlyn & Company, 2490 Trans Canada Highway, Mill Bay
Sundays, 10:00 am to 4:00 pm, from the first Sunday in May to the last Sunday in September
Contact: Lynne van der Have
Tel: (250) 743-4922
Fax: (250) 743-4288
caitlyn@wherecooksshop.com

Produce, baked goods and chicken from nearby Engeler Farm, Arbutus Ridge Farms, Kilrenny Farm and Merridale House Sourdough Breads.

Sundays took on a whole new palette when the Frayne Market started up last year in Mill Bay. The market perfectly complements its neighbours, The Coffee Mill, that sells "serious" organic coffee and delicious treats, and Caitlyn & Company, the ultimate cooks' cookshop.

Caitlyn & Company owner Lynne van der Have welcomes the growers, who include Mara Jernigan of Engeler Farm. Mara often teaches cooking classes at the store, as does Noël Richardson of Ravenhill Herb Farm and caterer Jenny Cameron.

Lynne says her customers "tend to be well educated and well travelled, with pretty sophisticated palates, so they really appreciate being able to

buy local, just-picked veggies here." Throughout the market months, Lynne offers food preparation tips and demonstrations using the market fresh produce.

GABRIOLA FARMERS' MARKET

Gabriola Agricultural Association grounds on South Road, ¼ mile up the hill from the ferry dock (ferry to Nanaimo)
Saturdays, 10:00 am to 12:00 noon, from the May long weekend to the Thanksgiving weekend
Contact: Tannie Meyer
Tel: (250) 247-8216
Fax: (250) 247-7251
ebus87@island.net

Mostly organic growers including Gabriola Gourmet Garlic, Meyer Farm, Heavenly Flowers and Good Heart Vegetables, Auld Alliance Farm, Gabriola Greenhouse, Freedom Farm, Berry Point Fruit and Honey and Early Dawn. Homemade bread and baked goods, vinegars, eggs, and crafts. There is a full-service kitchen.

Tannie Meyer looks back fondly to when the Gabriola Farmers' Market started up in 1995, "with six people standing under a tarp in the pouring rain." It has literally exploded since then, with 80-plus stalls, and a good-natured parking problem!

The Board of Directors of the Gabriola Agricultural Society runs the market. Tannie sets it all up every year, taking reservations for the 60 regular stalls and making a list of "casuals," who fill in at the other stalls when they have something to sell. The board hires a manager once the market is under way, as most of its directors are also vendors.

JAMES BAY COMMUNITY MARKET

Corner of Menzies and Superior streets (behind the Legislative Buildings)
Saturdays, 9:00 am to 3:00 pm, May to September (often stays open into October)
Tel: 381-5323
www.jamesbaymarket.com

Natural. 45 vendors, 75% of which are crafts and 25% produce, including Cathy Beech of Beech Lake Farm, Jason Smith, "the pepper man," and Connie Ferreira, whose wild flower arrangements stop traffic on Menzies Street.

The James Bay Community Market really does have that country market feel, even though it's located on a busy city street. It must be the grass underfoot, and the many special touches such as local buskers, and agricultural contests including "best pie" and "biggest zucchini" held throughout the season. There are special event days, too, from Emily Carr Day and The Garden Party to an alternative Health Show and Fall Fair.

Former chair of the James Bay Market Society Pat McGuire says the market "encourages healthy growing practices and wants nothing grown with pesticides." The society gives free space to local non-profit groups wanting to raise awareness of their programs and causes, and Pat says there is a great sense of community at the market. "It really is a place where people can come and gather, buy and sell, and create awareness about local economic sustainability."

MARKET-IN-THE-PARK

Centennial Park, Ganges, Salt Spring Island
Saturdays, 8:30 am to 3:30 pm, first Saturday in April to last Saturday in October
Contact: CRD Parks and Recreation
Tel: (250) 537-4448
www.saltspringmarket.com

Produce, baked goods, cheese, crafts. You'll find a number of familiar faces, from David Wood of Salt Spring Island Cheese Company, Susan and Julia Grace of Moonstruck Organic Cheese, Rosalie Beach of Wave Hill Farm, Heather Campbell – The Bread Lady, Harry Burton and Debbie McNamara of Apple Luscioius Organic Orchard and Craig Leitch and Beverley Stewart of Fern Creek Farm.

Nothing epitomizes the Salt Spring Island lifestyle more than the Saturday market. The 1970s may have come and gone, but this market remains a true "happening," with every kind of produce, food, objets d'art and crafts for sale. When the Capital Regional District took over the market management in 1996, they introduced a "make it, bake it, or grow it" policy.

With over 120 vendors at the peak summer season, market coordinator Jennifer Demery calls this "The place to be. Market-in-the-Park is really the pulse of the Island; it's more than just people selling, it's people meeting, music, information. Many non-profit groups raise awareness at the market, from the conservancy trying to preserve our old growth forests to the Raging Grannies. Children are allowed to set up in the middle

of the market for free, and they have a great time selling everything from paintings to gumboots filled with earth and flowers."

Salt Spring Island also has a very small organic produce farmers' market held at 112 Hereford Avenue on Tuesday mornings, which has a loyal local following. Charlie Eagle of Bright Farm is the organizer. Tel: (250) 537-4319.

METCHOSIN FARMERS' MARKET

On the municipal grounds behind the fire hall on Happy Valley Road, Metchosin

From Mother's Day in May to mid-October, Sundays, 11:00 am to 2:00 pm, special Harvest Festival Day in the fall

Contact: Dieter Eisenhawer

Tel: 474-7161

diesenhawer@pacificcoast.net

Mainly produce including Umi Nami Farm, Two Wings Farm, Eisenhawer Organic Produce, Swallow Hill Farm, Single Hill Farm, bread from Nature's Gifts and honey from Quails' Roost Farm.

Dieter Eisenhawer of Eisenhawer Organic Produce is one of those indefatigable volunteers who seems to do everything, including running the Metchosin Farmers' Market. He says he became president of the Metchosin Producers' Association by default, and is now responsible for organizing the 30 or so local farmers who participate in the market.

This real country market started up ten years ago, and was originally held in front of the community hall. There are 15 to 18 stalls at every market, and a loyal customer base from Colwood and Langford, plus a good sprinkling of city folk like myself.

At the Harvest Festival, local musicians and clowns set the stage, and the highlight is a rooster crowing contest. People are asked to guess the time when the rooster is going to crow, and the person who comes closest to the time wins a produce voucher.

MOSS STREET MARKET

Corner of Moss Street and Fairfield Road (Sir James Douglas School)

Saturdays, 10:00 am to 2:00 pm, May to late October

Contact: Jackie Robson

Tel: 361-9446

Produce, flowers, preserves, doughnuts, sausages, crafts. Among the many: ALM Organic Farm, Umi Nami Farm, Eisenhawer Organic Produce, Moonstruck Organic Cheese, Elk Lake Farm, Rebecca's Organic Garden, Redwing Organic Farm, Llewellyn Spring Organic Farm and Lynburn Farm.

Victoria's flagship organic farmers' market is living proof that location isn't everything. The Moss Street Market has been held at four locations that I remember, and no move ever diminished the crowd of regulars who show up long before the bell is struck at 10:00 o'clock.

Mary Alice Johnson of ALM Organic Farm was one of the founders in 1992, and is still active on its board, and as a vendor. She loves the healthy buzz there on Saturdays, especially the conversations with customers. "What are you going to do with that?" she asks, and recipes and culinary advice are exchanged.

The Moss Street merchants take their wares indoors for a lively Christmas market in early December.

NEW DUNCAN FARMERS' MARKET

Trunk Road and Canada Avenue, near the train station in Duncan
Saturdays, 9:00 to 1:00 pm, March to December (lots of special Christmas fare on the four Saturdays in December)
Contact: Steve Miller
Tel: (250) 743-7055
shadybrook@home.com

Mainly Natural market gardeners including Valerie's Organic Seed Garlic, Yellow Point Orchards, Bensons' Olde Tyme Farm, The Community Farm Store, Shadybrook Farm, Perennial Ridge Farms and Hard to Come By Farm.

Vendor Rose Rogan, who takes her perennial plants to market from Perennial Ridge Farm, loves the "really neat feeling" of the New Duncan Farmers' Market. She feels it "really represents the valley" with up to 60 stalls of local produce, food products, flowers and crafts, and I agree. There is a nice community feeling, a sense that people are dependent on the smallholders who bring their wares to market.

Steve Miller, another vendor and past president of the Board of the Cowichan Valley Small Holders Society, says he enjoys "the excitement of finding interesting and healthy foods, and seeing what's going to be there each week." He reminds me that farming is hard, isolating work and the market re-energizes him. At "the social event of the week," he enjoys chatting with the other producers and comparing notes. Ultimately, though,

it's the customers who mean the most. "Our customers are so supportive and appreciative, and we do feel we are making a positive contribution to their health and well being, particularly the seniors. If someone doesn't show up on market day, we always check on them."

The New Duncan Farmers' Market has been operating for seven years. The "new" part refers to the newest incarnation of markets held at this location for maybe a hundred years. If you're looking for the market, locals will direct you to its landmark. "The mound" is that big hump of land covered in trees at the back of the market. There are both covered and open stalls, and lively local entertainment including Eugene Smith who plays blues guitar and harmonica, and the irrepressible Acoustic Stew.

PENINSULA COUNTRY MARKET

1528 Stelly's Cross Road (Agricultural Fair Grounds)
From mid-June to the Thanksgiving weekend in October, Saturdays, 9:00 am to 1:00 pm
Contact: Jim Crawford
Tel: 360-1314
or Shari Griffin
Tel: 216-0521

Half produce, half crafts including Friss Farm, New Forest Apiaries, and Hazelmere Farm and a farmers' co-operative stall which benefits the local 4-H Club.

Now in its tenth year, the Peninsula Country Market draws "an awfully big pile of people," says Jim Crawford. When Jim isn't organizing the 50-plus vendors, he can be found making and selling brightly painted whirly-gigs for the garden.

There's entertainment every market day, which, together with the fairground location and great choice of things to buy, adds up to a great country experience.

SIDNEY SUMMER MARKET

Beacon Avenue, Sidney between Second Street and Fifth Street
Thursdays, 5:30 to 8:30 pm, in the summer months
Contact: Reg Teeney
Tel: 655-1808
or Brenda Milne
Tel: 656-1910

Organic produce from local farms including Beech Farm, Friss Farm and Elk Lake Farms, organic bread and baked goods, arts and crafts.

This is a real old-fashioned market, with everything from face painting to fresh, local produce to cotton candy. The main street transforms into a kind of weekly community festival where locals and visitors mingle, look, buy and enjoy the music. Sidney's weekly entertainment has included local bands and a troupe of belly dancers. Reg Teeney says one couple visiting from Boston, "enjoyed the market so much that they actually skipped Butchart Gardens to enjoy the fun!"

The market is two years young, and already attracts 150 vendors, and over 20,000 buyers annually. The local merchants get in on the act, too, with sidewalk sales.

Money raised from stall fees goes back into the local community in the form of grants.

SOOKE COUNTRY MARKET

Turn right onto Otter Point Road at Sooke's only set of lights. The market is held on the grassy lot.

From Mother's Day in May to Labour Day Weekend in September, Saturdays, 10:00 am to 2:00 pm.

Contact: Melanie Derksen

Tel: 642-4687

melderk@home.com

There are 8 to 15 stalls depending on the season. Produce, crafts, organic honey, baked goods and preserves. You'll find Quails' Roost Farm, Single Hill Farm, Singing Frog Farm, and Ladybird Farm.

With strong local support, and lots of visiting Victorians and tourists, the Sooke Country Market has been well established for six years. Melanie Derksen says "Locals love to come out for the local organic produce" and those vendors are always very busy when the bell rings at 10 o'clock.

There is a featured artists' program, which provides a wonderful forum for a different local artist to exhibit each month. Children are well taken care of in a special tent, and often, one of Sooke's noted wandering minstrels will entertain.

Melanie is a market gardener, who uses organic methods and says she doesn't "know of any other way to grow" for her own family. When she has a surplus, she takes it to market, along with her jams and preserves that are often purchased by the many local bed-and-breakfast operators.

Chapter Six: Cultivated Dining

LOCAL RESTAURANTS THAT HAVE CHOSEN ORGANIC OR ARE
SERIOUSLY HEADING THAT WAY

I try to eat only organics, I love to eat out, and I'm happy to report that the two are not mutually exclusive. People often ask me where to eat as organically as possible in and around Victoria, and the answers lie in this chapter.

As there aren't any completely certified organic restaurants here, the secret is to do your research before you dine. And, if you think a restaurant could do better, speak to your server, chat to the chef or owner, and always fill out those customer surveys that ask for suggestions (I do!). The more people who demand organic produce, meat and poultry, the better off we will all be: growers, restaurateurs and consumers.

You'll find that many local chefs are actively seeking organic produce for its taste, texture and health benefits, and because customers are asking more questions before they order. Is the salmon wild? Are the vegetables organic? Which organic wines do you serve? Farm Folk/City Folk and the Island Chefs' Collaborative have been huge influences on the use of organics by restaurants and caterers, and you'll find that most chefs who eat organically themselves endeavour to bring the same sensibility to their menus.

THE AERIE RESORT

600 Ebadora Lane
P.O. Box 108
Malahat V0R 2L0
Tel: (250) 743-7115
Fax: (250) 743-4766
www.aerie.bc.ca
aerie@relaischateaux.fr
Natural
French with Pacific Northwest influence
Owner: Maria Schuster
General Manager: Markus Griesser
Executive Chef: Christophe Letard

CULTIVATED DINING

Open year round, Monday to Sunday, lunch: 12:00 noon, 12:30 pm, 1:00 pm and 1:30 pm seatings; dinner served from 6:00 pm, last seating at 9:00 pm

One marvels at the calibre of restaurants now available to south island residents. The Aerie Resort, a Mediterranean-style villa located atop the Malahat, is part of the Relais et Château Group, no less, and an AAA Four Diamond and Mobil Four Diamond Award winner.

Dining is an important part of The Aerie Resort experience. Christophe Letard takes full advantage of the abundance of locally grown products from the Cowichan Valley and Vancouver Island, from seafood to game to fresh morels and berries. Every dining experience includes the opportunity to meet with Chef Letard prior to dinner for his daily menu discussion.

Letard began cooking at the family farm in France, where he helped his mother prepare meals for his six older brothers. He trained at the Hotel Savoie Leman, France's oldest cooking school, and was part of the team at La Ferme St. Simeon in Honfleur when it received its first Michelin star. At the Inn at Manitou in Ontario, Letard learned to cook using styles from around the world, but incorporating local flavours. He began as sous chef at The Aerie Resort, taking over as executive chef in March 2000. With a brigade of 14, Letard serves the resort's 75-seat restaurant.

WARM SALAD OF COBBLE HILL WHITE ASPARAGUS AND WEATHERVANE SCALLOPS

Christophe Letard, The Aerie Resort
Makes 4 individual-sized salads.

Salad

8 LARGE SCALLOPS
12 WHITE ASPARAGUS
1 LEMON
RICE WINE VINEGAR
1 TBSP BALSAMIC VINEGAR*
1 SMALL BAG MÂCHE LETTUCE
OIL FOR COOKING
SALT AND FRESHLY GROUND BLACK PEPPER

Lemongrass Syrup and Georgie's Rhubarb Relish

1 LEMONGRASS STICK, CHOPPED FINE
2 OZ HONEY
1 LEMON, JUICED

4 RHUBARB STICKS, CHOPPED IN SMALL BRUNOISE (SMALL DICE)

SALT AND PEPPERCORN

THYME, BAY LEAF AND CLOVE

*Chef Letard uses Venturi Schultze balsamic vinegar

In a small stainless steel pan, bring to boil the lemongrass, honey, lemon juice, thyme, bay leaf, clove and 1 cup of water. Simmer and reduce by half. Strain and put this syrup back into the pan. Add the rhubarb. Simmer again for 5 minutes, until the rhubarb is soft. Remove from heat, cool down and reserve. Peel the white asparagus without damaging the heads. Finely shave 4 of the asparagus. Place them in a bowl and pour some of the lemon juice from the relish on them, plus a touch of rice vinegar. Set aside. Add the lemon juice to some salted boiling water and cook the remaining white asparagus until tender. Keep the asparagus warm. Season the scallops and sear them on both sides until golden brown and warm inside. Place 2 scallops on each of 4 plates. Add two asparagus on top of each plate. In a bowl, mix the asparagus shavings with some mâche lettuce, seasoned with a little bit of the relish. Place a nice dome of the salad on top of the scallops and finish the plate with some of the relish around on the plate and a few drops of balsamic vinegar.

SILVERSIDE FARM BLACKBERRY JAM AND DARK CHOCOLATE GANACHE TART WITH ORANGE MARINATED COBBLE HILL FRESH BLUEBERRIES AND BLACKBERRIES AND GRAND MARNIER, COX APPLE JUICE AND VANILLA POD SYRUP

Christophe Letard, The Aerie Resort
Makes 4 individual-sized tarts.

Sweet Dough

9 OZ FLOUR

3 OZ SUGAR

⅓ LB BUTTER

1 EGG

Jam

1 PINT BLACKBERRIES

1 PINT SUGAR

JUICE FROM 1 LEMON

Dark Chocolate Ganache

10 OZ BITTERSWEET CHOCOLATE CHIPS

4 OZ BUTTER

5 oz whipped cream
2 tbsp Grand Marnier

Marinated Berries

juice and zest from 2 oranges
4 tbsp honey
½ pint berries
2 tbsp Grand Marnier

Syrup

juice from 8 Cox apples, or ½ litre apple juice
1 vanilla pod
½ oz Grand Marnier
1 oz sugar

Make the sweet dough, jam and syrup the day before. First mix the sugar and butter together. Add the flour and mix together. Add the egg and form a ball. Cover it and leave to rest. Make the jam. Bring to boil with 1 cup of water the blackberries, lemon juice and sugar. Cook for 15 minutes, simmering, and reserve. Make the syrup. Bring the apple juice to boil with the vanilla pod (slit open lengthwise), Grand Marnier and sugar. Reduce to a syrup or to the equivalent of 16 tbsp of liquid. Reserve. The next day, preheat oven to 300°F. Roll the dough into four, 3-inch moulds and bake for 20 minutes or until light golden. Pour 2 tbsp of the jam into shells and reserve. Make the ganache. Boil the whipped cream and pour on the chocolate and diced butter. Whisk until the mixture is smooth. Add the Grand Marnier and pour into the shells to fill them up. Let the shells stand in a cool place. Marinate the berries. Boil up all the ingredients except the berries. Let this syrup cool down for 15 minutes and pour it on the berries. Reserve. Place the tart on the centre of the plate. Display some of the berries on top. Pour some of the syrup around and finish with fresh mint.

BEAN AROUND THE WORLD

533 Fisgard Street
Victoria V8W 1R3
Tel: 386-7115
Fax: 370-0370
beans@island.net
Certified Organic
Coffee shop
Owners: Maureen Gardin and Mike Garnett

Open Monday to Saturday, 8:00 am to 6:00 pm, Sunday, 9:00 am to 6:00 pm

One doesn't need to go around the world to appreciate the cosy European Kaffeehaus atmosphere of this family-operated establishment. Tucked in to a 19th-century building in the heart of Chinatown, Maureen and Mike's coffee shop attracts an eclectic crowd, young and old.

Of the 26 kinds of coffee on offer, 22 are certified organic. Says Maureen, "As a coffee-shop owner, I don't understand why more people aren't doing it — we pay only a few cents more a pound for organic."

She and Mike started the shop five years ago, and there was organic on tap from day one. They're supplied by Mike's best friend, who owns the Bean Around the World Coffee company in Vancouver. Pastries are supplied fresh daily by Patisserie Daniel, Cascadia Bakery, Sally and John's Place, and soups come in from the local Vancouver Island Soup Company.

Maureen believes organics should be supported worldwide. She says hearing that coffee workers' rubber gloves are literally melting off their hands because of the chemicals on conventional plantations is enough for her to encourage everyone to champion organic farming.

CAFÉ BRIO

944 Fort Street
Victoria V8V 3K2
Tel: 383-0009
Fax: 383-0063
www.cafebrio.com
Certified Organic
Contemporary West Coast
Owners: Sylvia Marcolini and Greg Hayes
Chef: Sean Brennan

Open daily for dinner from 5:30 pm, for lunch from April through the fall, 12:00 noon to 2:30 pm. Usually closed December 24 to 26, and for the first week of January.

Maybe I'm just getting old, but I am continually struck by how young the new chefs are, and also, in the case of Sean Brennan, how committed. Even a particularly hectic day didn't stop him from taking a sincere interest in this book, and it's obvious that organics are dear to his heart, professionally and personally. He eats organically and enjoys visiting local farms on his days off.

When we met, he was producing a labour plan for the year and calmly fielding calls from suppliers. He deals with over ten organic suppliers including Lynburn Farm, Cowichan Bay Farm, Engeler Farm, Two Wings Farm and Ragley Farm. Lynburn's Tina Fraser has supplied Café Brio since it opened, and Sean meets regularly with her to pore over seed catalogues. With the menu in mind, they decide together what will be planted. It's typical of the close relationships that have developed between local chefs and growers. Each time Tina delivers vegetables, she picks up compost from the kitchen for her farm. "We've recently also sent our wild fish refuse," says Sean, "and she tells me all the good enzymes and bacteria are really heating up her compost pile!"

Sean says it's important for restaurants to ensure produce is certified organic, and to develop personal relationships with the growers. "We need to know we can trust the produce because there are just too many problems, like BSE." As chair of the Island Chefs' Collaborative, Sean is pleased that many other local restaurants are taking the time to search out organic suppliers.

Sean trained in Vancouver, worked at The Raintree restaurant there, and then came to Harvest Moon in Victoria. When Greg and Sylvia created their delicious, vivacious hideaway on Fort Street, Sean took over the kitchen, and the rest is organic history in the making. In winter, nothing is more inviting than the art-smart, deep Tuscan yellow and rust interior; in summer, heaven is lingering over supper on the wisteria-fringed patio.

CREAMED CHANTERELLES WITH BACON AND SAGE ON GRILLED BREAD

Sean Brennan, Café Brio
Makes 4 servings.

4 SLICES OF GOOD COUNTRY-STYLE BREAD, CUT INTO ¾"-1" THICKNESS
1 CLOVE GARLIC, PEELED AND CUT IN HALF
4 C CHANTERELLES, CLEANED AND, IF LARGE, HALVED OR QUARTERED
2 TBSP BUTTER
2 SHALLOTS, PEELED AND FINELY DICED
3 STRIPS OF NATURAL SMOKED BACON
1½ TBSP FRESH SAGE, CHOPPED
1 C CHICKEN STOCK
¾ C WHOLE CREAM
1 TBSP LEMON JUICE
4 FRESH SAGE TIPS FOR GARNISH

Grill the bread over hot coals until it is nicely toasted, or toast under a broiler in the oven. Rub one side of the bread with the garlic, set aside and keep warm.

In a large sauté pan, render the bacon of its fat and drain on paper towels. Clean the pan, then melt the butter and gently sauté the shallots until translucent. Add the chanterelles, turn the heat up to medium, season with salt and pepper, and cook until all mushroom juices have evaporated. Add the chicken stock, reduce liquid by ¾, then add the cream, sage and bacon. Reduce the sauce to a creamy consistency (not too thick), and stir in the lemon juice. Place a slice of the grilled bread in the centre of each of 4 warmed plates, spoon the mushrooms evenly on top of the bread and spoon the sauce around the bread and mushrooms. Garnish with the sage tips.

CONFIT OF DUCK
Sean Brennan, Café Brio

12 PIECES OF DUCK LEGS, TRIMMED OF ANY EXTRA FAT
3 OZ (BY VOLUME) ROCK SALT
¼ C PEPPERCORNS
¼ BULB GARLIC, PEELED AND SLICED THIN
1 BUNCH FRESH THYME
1 BAY LEAF, CRUSHED
2 LITRES RENDERED DUCK FAT, MELTED

Preheat oven to 275°F. Mix together all of the above ingredients, and place in a non-reactive (e.g., glass) container. Cover, and place in fridge for 48 hours; then remove and wipe the duck pieces clean. Place the duck pieces in a large pot and cover with the melted duck fat. Cook in oven for 4-6 hours, or until very tender to the touch. Remove the duck pieces from the pot and crisp the skin under broiler, or cool legs and fat separately, then pour fat back over legs to completely cover, and refrigerate until needed.

Sean's note: "Serve the confit with various seasonal accompaniments such as sweet potato purée, Anjou pear and grilled endive with a balsamic reduction, or with a lentil and roast beet salad, or with grilled asparagus and morel mushroom ragout."

ISLAND CHEFS' COLLABORATIVE (ICC)
Mission Statement

"The Island Chefs' Collaborative is a non-profit group comprised of progressive chefs dedicated to promoting Vancouver Island cuisine. The ICC stands for an ethical approach to food

CULTIVATED DINING

and a commitment to locally-grown, high-quality ingredients. We are passionate about good food. We believe that food nourishes us both in body and soul, and that the sharing of food immeasurably enriches our sense of community. We believe that good food begins with unpolluted air, land, and water, and is dependent on environmentally-sustainable farming and fishing. We are frustrated with the abundance of mass-produced and toxic foodstuffs overwhelming today's marketplace; in response, we emphasise locally-grown, organic, seasonal, and minimally-processed ingredients. We support growers and producers who rely on sustainable farming practices, and we are committed to utilizing their products by educating our customers to help to further their efforts."

MEMBERS

Member restaurants include Café Brio, The Marina Restaurant, The Empress Room, Cassis, The Aerie Resort, Camille's, Willie's Bakery and Market Café and Zambri's, and caterers such as Feys & Hobbs and Truffles Catering Group.

The whole idea is to support the local farmers. Sean Brennan of Café Brio says chefs in the collaborative choose Vancouver Island certified organic, organic and then conventional in that order, before going farther afield for produce. The ICC holds fundraising and "awareness-raising" events throughout the year.

Contact: Sue Bielert

Tel: 381-8865

moss@islandnet.com

CAMILLE'S

45 Bastion Square
Victoria V8W 1J1
Tel: 381-3433
Fax: 381-3403
www.camillesrestaurant.com
camilles@pacificcoast.net
Certified Organic, Transitional and Natural
West Coast/International
Owners: David Mincey and Paige Robinson
Chef: Joe Warde

Open daily for dinner, weekdays: 5:30 pm to 9:00 pm (weekdays), weekends: 5:30 pm to 10:00 pm

Camille's is a cosy, romantic restaurant tucked into the 1899 Law Chambers building in historic Bastion Square. The cuisine is based on the harvests of many local organic growers and suppliers. Co-owner David Mincey is proud to have "built up a network of Island producers who provide most of what turns up on our menus, which change every two weeks."

Complementing the cuisine is a large, award-winning wine list emphasizing vintners from Vancouver Island and other parts of British Columbia. Tasting dinners and wine-appreciation classes are often held in the restaurant—call or visit the web site for a schedule.

"As members of the Island Chefs' Collaborative, we strive to support local organic producers and suppliers," says David. "By purchasing from small local growers, we are attempting to make organic gardening a viable economic reality for our farmers, hopefully encouraging more farmers to go the organic route."

SALAD OF HEIRLOOM TOMATOES AND BLUE CORN CAKES WITH GARLIC CUSTARD

Joe Warde, Camille's
Makes 36 corn cakes.

ASSORTED SLICED HEIRLOOM TOMATOES (ALLOW ½-1 C TOMATOES PER SERVING)
3 WHOLE HEADS (BULBS) GARLIC
1 C EXTRA VIRGIN OLIVE OIL
1 C 35% CREAM
3 EGGS
3 C YELLOW CORNMEAL
2 C BLUE CORNMEAL
3 C UNBLEACHED FLOUR
1 C SUGAR
6 TBSP BAKING POWDER
1 TSP SALT
4 EGGS
4 C MILK
GARLIC OIL (RESERVED FROM THE BAKING PAN)

Preheat oven to 350°F. Slice tops off the garlic heads, place in small baking dish and drizzle the olive oil over. Cover the dish and bake until garlic is soft, approximately 30 minutes. Reserve the oil from baking dish, squeeze garlic out of the skins, blend with the 3 eggs and cream until smooth. Season with salt and pepper. In a large bowl, mix the cornmeals, flour, baking powder, sugar and salt. Combine the 4 eggs with the milk, and stir lightly into the dry

ingredients. Add 2 tbsp of the reserved garlic oil. Do not over-mix. Pour into greased muffin tins. Place a teaspoonful of the garlic custard mixture into the centre of each muffin and bake for 20-25 minutes, until golden. Toss the sliced tomatoes in some of the reserved garlic oil and season with sea salt. Slice the warm muffins and serve with the tomato salad.

Joe's note: "This makes about 36 muffins. Save the extra for another dish or freeze and eat later!"

THE DINING ROOM AT DUNSMUIR LODGE

1515 McTavish Road
Sidney V8L 3Y3
Tel: 656-3166
Fax: 656-1999
www.reservations@dunsmuirlodge.com
dunsmuir@uvic.ca
Certified Organic and Natural
Pactific Northwest (casual dining in the Peninsula Lounge and informal fine dining in the Main Dining Room)
Owner: The University of Victoria
Food and Beverage Manager: Liam Morton
Chef: Candace Hartley

Open year-round, Monday to Sunday, breakfast 7:00 to 9:00 am, lunch 11:45 am to 1:00 pm, dinner 5:30 to 8:30 pm. Closed Christmas Day and New Year's Day.

Dining at Dunsmuir Lodge has always had a certain cachet. It's a destination restaurant, and one drives from Victoria along West Saanich Road with great anticipation. I suppose it is partly the setting, the view and the sense of privacy, and partly the restaurant's reputation for focussing on what's in season.

Says Candace Hartley, "We have many local farmers who grow interesting organic produce for us, so our menu changes daily to reflect this. I believe in serving unique food that tastes great! Therefore, I like to encourage local growers to produce unusual organic products which are not necessarily products that most diners would recognize."

In Toronto, Hartley trained at the Windsor Arms Hotel, attended George Brown College, worked at L'Hotel and Sutton Place before heading west

to The Empress Hotel. She has cooked for many prestigious wine and food events including the Invitational Collaborative Chefs Dinners in Toronto, Hawaii and California.

SALT SPRING ISLAND GOAT CHEESE AND MASCARPONE BLINTZES WITH DRIED FRUIT COMPOTE

Candace Hartley, The Dining Room at Dunsmuir Lodge
Makes 12-14 blintzes.

Crepes

2 LARGE EGGS
½ C WATER
½ C PLUS 2 TBSP MILK
1 C FLOUR
PINCH OF SALT
1 OZ (¼ STICK) MELTED SWEET BUTTER

In a stainless steel bowl, whisk together the eggs, water and ½ cup of the milk. Add the flour and salt and stir in the butter. Refrigerate the batter for at least ½ hour to overnight, and then strain it. To make the crepes, heat a 6" non-stick or seasoned crepe pan over medium heat. Pour 2 tbsp of the batter into the pan and quickly rotate the pan, spreading a thin layer of batter over the entire bottom. Cook the crepe for a couple of minutes until golden brown. Invert the crepe with the edge of a knife or your fingers. Cook the other side for about 30 seconds. Invert the pan to release the crepe. Proceed to make the rest of the crepes in the same manner, stacking them as you make them.

Candace's note: "If your first few crepes are too thick, thin the batter out with the extra milk."

Filling

8 OZ MASCARPONE
8 OZ SALT SPRING ISLAND GOAT CHEESE
3 TBSP SUGAR
1 LEMON, ZESTED (RESERVE JUICE FOR THE COMPOTE)
3 OZ DRIED APRICOTS, JUILLIENNED AND POACHED IN RIESLING OR ICE WINE (OPTIONAL)
2 OZ DRIED CRANBERRIES, POACHED IN RIESLING OR ICE WINE (OPTIONAL)

In a bowl, mix the filling ingredients together. Place two tablespoons of filling in the middle of each crepe, fold the ends of the crepe into the middle and roll crepe into a neat bundle. This may be done several hours ahead, or the day before.

Compote

1 C DRIED APRICOTS, DICED
2 PEARS, DICED
¾ C DRIED CRANBERRIES
½ C HONEY
1 C RIESLING OR ICE WINE
1 LEMON, ZESTED
1 C BLUEBERRIES
1 OZ GRATED GINGER
JUICE OF 2 LEMONS
4 OZ UNSALTED BUTTER

Simmer apricots, pears, cranberries, honey, wine, lemon zest and ginger together in a non-reactive sauce pan until apricots are tender (10 minutes). Remove fruit from juice, simmer until juices reduce by half, and whisk in butter. Add blueberries.

To serve, warm up the pre-filled blintzes by gently pan-frying in clarified butter for one or two minutes. Place one or two blintzes on each plate, and drizzle compote over. Alternatively, serve compote separately to be spooned over at the table.

THE EMPRESS ROOM

The Empress Hotel
721 Government Street
Victoria V8W 1W5
Tel: 384-8111
Fax: 389-2736
www.fairmont.com
david.hammonds@fairmont.com
scott.baechler@fairmont.com
Certified Organic, Transitional and Natural
West Coast Fine Dining
Executive Chef: David Hammonds
Executive Sous Chef: Scott Baechler

Open daily for dinner, 6:00 to 9:30 pm. Closed from the first week of January to the second week of February.

Scott Baechler enthuses about the "public's increased interest in knowing what they're eating and where it comes from," and the importance of "more intimate relationships developing between farmers and

professionals." A recent case in point was his and Chef Hammonds' decision to present only Salt Spring Island cheeses, the result of their inspiring visits to Salt Sprint Island Cheese Company and Moonstruck Organic Cheese. David Wood and Julia Grace have reciprocated with an education session for The Empress Room staff, and now the restaurant's cheese course is refreshingly local and organic, not to mention delicious.

Chef Hammonds, who steered the hotel's four restaurants through their major 1989 restoration, says it is only in recent years that customers have taken a keen interest in what they're eating. He says The Empress Room sells more chicken breasts when they're organic, and he knows to serve only wild fish. He believes that people should be provided with the best ingredients, and he regularly purchases organics from ProOrganics, Hills and Albion Fisheries. Saanichton's Gavin's Fresh Herbs is responsible for the herbs and expressive flower garnishes, and a number of other farmers bring their harvests to the kitchen door.

Hammonds apprenticed at the famed Gleneagles Hotel, Scotland, was a member of the opening team for Toronto's King Edward Hotel and Executive Chef of Whistler's Delta Mountain Inn. Baechler came to The Empress Room via Toronto's King Edward Hotel, Banff's Rimrock Resort and The Four Seasons, Nevis. Chatting with them over a first-rate cappuccino in the vast Empress kitchens, I could see why every plate they present in The Empress Room sings. Their passion is one of the main ingredients, and there is a nice symbiosis here, between farmer, chef and customer.

CULTIVATED DINING

ORGANIC SALT SPRING ISLAND GOAT CHEESE TART

Scott Baechler, The Empress Room
Makes 8-10 servings.

Crust

1½ C ALL-PURPOSE FLOUR
5 OZ UNSALTED BUTTER (AT ROOM TEMPERATURE)
4 TSP SUGAR
1 TBSP WATER
¼ TSP SALT
½ TSP VANILLA EXTRACT

Place the flour, sugar, salt, and butter into a large mixing bowl. Blend in the butter until it is the size of peas. Add the water and vanilla extract. Stir until the dough forms one piece and there is no

dry flour. Gather the dough into a ball, wrap in plastic and chill for 30 minutes. Then, roll out on a floured surface to form a circle about ⅜" thick and 12" in diameter. Place the dough in a 10" or 12" pie pan, and chill until firm, about 20 minutes. Preheat oven to 425°F. Line the dough with foil and weigh it down with dried beans or rice. Place in the oven and bake for 20 minutes. Remove the beans or rice and foil, and continue to bake until lightly golden, about 5 minutes. Set aside to cool.

Filling

8 OZ GOAT CHEESE*
10 OZ GOOD QUALITY CREAM CHEESE (AT ROOM TEMPERATURE)
⅔ C SUGAR
2 EGGS, SEPARATED
2 EGG YOLKS
1 INCH VANILLA BEAN, SEEDS ONLY
PINCH OF SALT

*Scott uses Salt Spring Island Cheese Company's goat cheese

Preheat oven to 325°F. In a medium bowl or mixer, blend the cheeses until smooth (don't over-mix). Whisk in the sugar, then the 4 egg yolks and the vanilla bean seeds. In a very clean, cool bowl, whisk the egg whites with salt until soft firm peaks form. Fold this mixture into the cheese mixture in two batches. Pour the cheese-and-egg-white mixture into the pre-baked pie shell. Line the outer rim of cheese with thinly sliced fruit of your choice (pears or nectarines work well). Bake the tart for 40 minutes until set; then cool.

Scott's note: "Here is a great, sweet twist on organic goat cheese!"

FOSTER'S EATERY

753 Yates Street
Victoria V8W 1L6
Tel: 382-1131
Fax: 382-1187
Certified Organic and Natural
Artsy Bistro
Owner: Sean Sloat
Chef: Matthew Malcolm

Open Monday to Friday, 8:00 am to 3:00 pm for breakfast and lunch, dinner from 5:00 pm, Saturday brunch, 11:00 am to 3:00 pm, Sunday

brunch 10:00 am to 3:00 pm. Take-out and catering menus. Charming outdoor courtyard dining in summer.

In the middle of the lunchtime buzz, Sean Sloat calmly tells me how happy he is. It's a happiness that stems from a strong business plan, hard work and the belief that "it all comes down to caring about food, how a dish looks, how it tastes, and knowing one shouldn't take short-cuts — you get out what you put in."

Sean and Matthew Malcolm are careful to choose the best produce for their menus, including organic field greens and herbs for their expressive salads, Salt Spring Island Cheese Company goat cheese for the caramelized onion tart, and Salt Spring Roasting Company fair trade, organic coffee, which is always on tap. Sean says his choice of organic ingredients "is a standard that I want to set and offer to my customers."

The restaurant's creative fare has been called "artsy and affordable," with credit to Chef Malcolm, who cut his teeth at Herald Street Caffe, then did a stint at his family's Creole kitchens in Missouri before returning to Victoria to work in the kitchen of Government House, and finally, Foster's. Sean has a background in front-of-house service in Victoria and Vancouver at The Latch, Oak Bay Beach Hotel, Earl's, Starbuck's and The Marina Restaurant. Both make organics their personal choice at home, and wherever possible, at Foster's.

ROASTED WILD MUSHROOM LASAGNE
Matthew Malcolm, Foster's Eatery
Makes 6-8 servings.

10 LB ASSORTED WILD MUSHROOMS, CLEANED, LEFT WHOLE
½ C OLIVE OIL
½ C BALSAMIC VINEGAR
SALT AND FRESHLY GROUND BLACK PEPPER
½ C FRESH THYME
1 C WHITE WINE
1½ WHITE ONIONS, CHOPPED
5 CLOVES GARLIC, CHOPPED
¼ C FRESH BASIL
1 LB SPINACH
1 750-ML TUB RICOTTA
20 OZ SLICED MOZZARELLA
PRE-COOKED LASAGNE NOODLES
GRATED PARMESAN

Preheat oven to 425°F. On a large (or a couple of large) baking sheets, place the mushrooms. Sprinkle with the oil, balsamic vinegar, salt and pepper, ¼ cup of the thyme and the wine. Roast in oven. Remove mushrooms from oven and set aside 2 cups. Purée the rest of the mushrooms. In a large skillet, using a little olive oil, sauté half of the onions with the garlic, salt and pepper and the remaining ¼ cup thyme. Add the mushroom purée, combine, and remove from heat. In another skillet, using a little olive oil, sauté the other half of the onions, add the spinach and basil. Remove from heat and add the ricotta. In a 9" by 12" lasagne pan, layer the noodles, mushroom mixture, noodles, ricotta mixture, noodles, mushroom mixture, grated Parmesan (to taste), whole mushrooms, and finally, the mozzarella slices. Cover with foil, and bake for 25 to 30 minutes.

GREEN CUISINE

#5-560 Johnson Street
Victoria V8W 3C6
Tel: 385-1809
www.greencuisine.com
andy@greencuisine.com
Certified Organic and Transitional
100% Vegan
Owner: Andy Cunningham

Open daily, 10:00 am to 8:00 pm

Andy Cunningham believes in serving "good food that doesn't cost the earth," as well as supporting local organic farmers. His Green Cuisine Vegetarian Restaurant, a fixture for ten years in Victoria's Market Square, offers delicious, healthy meals from a self-service hot buffet, salad bar and dessert bar, all of which are made fresh daily from natural and organic ingredients.

The restaurant produces its own breads, desserts and bakery items using unrefined sweeteners and organic flours, and offers a large selection of freshly squeezed organic juices, smoothies and shakes, and organic fair-traded coffees, cappuccinos, teas and chai.

Andy has personally developed all of the restaurant's recipes, from cold salads to hot entrées and desserts. And there is a nice, caring feeling in the signs on every dish that list the ingredients used, so that those with food sensitivities or who follow restricted diets (e.g., vegan, macrobiotic, low-gluten, wheat-free, soy-free) always have several choices.

Andy says he is "constantly trying out new recipes and responding to customer requests, while striving to maintain a high standard of organic and unprocessed ingredients."

Andy produces some of those high quality ingredients himself: Sooke Soy Foods tofu, and Green Cuisine Supersoy soy milk, tempeh, baked tofu, seitan, mochi and amasake, all of which are available at Seed of Life, Thrifty Foods, Lifestyle Markets, Capers Community Market and Colwood House of Nutrition, to name a few outlets. For those interested in learning how to cook some of the great dishes on offer in the restaurant, there are interactive cooking classes — just call or email Green Cuisine for a schedule.

JAMAICAN STEW
Andy Cunningham, Green Cuisine
Makes 4-6 servings.

2 TBSP VEGETABLE OIL
1 MEDIUM ONION, SLICED IN HALF MOONS
1 CARROT, SLICED DIAGONALLY
1 RED PEPPER, SLICED IN STRIPS
2 CANS (3¼ C) COCONUT MILK
1 TSP TURMERIC
3 TBSP PATAK'S HOT CURRY PASTE
¼ - 1 TSP SALT, TO TASTE
½ C FRESH OR FROZEN PEAS
1 HEAD BROCCOLI, CUT INTO FLORETS
1 HEAD CAULIFLOWER, CUT INTO FLORETS
2 CUPS YAMS AND/OR SQUASH, PEELED AND CUT INTO CHUNKS

Sauté the onion in oil until browned, then add carrot and red pepper. Continue to sauté for 5 minutes. Add the coconut milk, turmeric, curry paste and salt. Bring to a boil over medium-high heat. Add the remaining vegetables, maintaining a simmer with the lid on, until tender. After at least 20-30 minutes, leave the stew to cool slightly, then serve over brown rice, accompanied with your choice of chutneys, papadum, chapati, and/or fresh cilantro.

Andy's note: "Enjoy!"

MALAHAT MOUNTAIN INN
265 Trans-Canada Highway
Malahat V0R 2L0
Tel: 478-1944
Fax: 478-1926
hospitality@telus.net
Certified Organic, Transitional and Natural
West Coast
Owner: Lyn Noseworthy
Manager: Doug Stewart
Chef: Micah Lloyd

Open daily for lunch and dinner, Sunday to Thursday, 11:00 am to 9:00 pm, Friday and Saturday, 11:00 am to 10:00 pm

Chef Lloyd was proffering Purple Basil Marinated Dungeness Crab at this year's Feast of Fields, and it was the taste of that delicate hors d'oeuvre which lured me soon afterward to the restaurant itself. Wasn't this the place we used to stop decades ago for thick hot chocolate on the way to Mount Washington? If it was, then it has taken an amazing turn.

Dinner here is an event, and it's not just the live jazz played by guys in tuxedos, although I did enjoy that classy touch. Doug Stewart credits the "eclectic food, warm atmosphere and fabulous views of the Saanich Inlet" with attracting full houses night after night.

Stewart believes in "serving the freshest ingredients. When available, the quality of organic food only enhances the complex flavours and tastes of our menu, and allows us to uphold our high quality standards." The restaurant draws on Malahat and Mill Bay organic growers for its vegetables, edible flowers and spring mixed greens, and also buys its poultry locally. Chef Lloyd has a natural flair in the kitchen. He worked previously at Pescatore's, Amelia Street Bistro and Vinsantos, and regards organic ingredients as integral to his menu's success.

THE MARINA RESTAURANT

1327 Beach Drive
Victoria V8S 2N4
Tel: 598-3826
Fax: 598-3014
www.marinarestaurant.com
marina@pinc.com
Certified Organic
Pacific Northwest
Owner: Robert Wright
Chef: Melbourne O'Brien

Open daily, lunch: 11:00 am to 3:00 pm, dinner: 5:00 to 11:00 pm;
catering and banquet planning available

The only thing that's never changed at The Marina Restaurant is its spectacular sea view. Everything else has just gotten better. With the major renovation in 1994 came a shift to more contemporary fine dining and an emphasis on the use of fresh, natural ingredients.

Chef O'Brien supports the local farming community by regularly "using heirloom products not available in the consumer marketplace" and "sourcing and supporting local poultry and meat suppliers of antibiotic-free, free-range products." You'll find greens from Kildara Farm, produce from ALM Organic Farm, duck from the Cowichan Valley, exclusive crottin from the Salt Spring Island Cheese Company, Moonstruck Organic Cheese, and organic farmed salmon from Yellow Island Aquaculture on Quadra Island.

O'Brien, who says he is a "saucier by trade" gave me a fascinating cook's tour of his kitchen, stopping beside a tantalizing pot of veal stock to answer my questions about his career. He worked previously at the acclaimed Pan Pacific's Five Sails Restaurant in Vancouver, and was a member of the opening team for Château Whistler under Chef Bernard Casavant, a noted proponent of local organic ingredients. Arriving in Victoria two years ago, he was delighted to find such a vast network of market gardeners and organic suppliers, but feels there is still "a lot of public awareness needed" to bring organics into the restaurant mainstream.

I've enjoyed O'Brien's unique flattened chicken — accompanied by that great view — on many occasions and was delighted when he offered the recipe for this book.

FLATTENED CHICKEN WITH LEMON AND GARLIC CONFIT AND PORTOBELLO MUSHROOM WILD RICE TURNOVER

Melbourne O'Brien, The Marina Restaurant
Makes 2 servings.

1 LARGE PORTOBELLO MUSHROOM, FINELY DICED
2 TBSP FINELY DICED ZUCCHINI
2 TBSP FINELY DICED ONION
2 TBSP FINELY DICED CARROT
2 TBSP FINELY DICED CELERY
2 TBSP CRÈME FRAICHE OR SOUR CREAM
½ C COOKED WILD RICE
A PINCH OF CHOPPED FINE HERBS (PARSLEY, THYME, TARRAGON)
2 PÂTÉ BRISÉE ROUNDS, EACH 5" ACROSS AND ¼" THICK*
8 CLOVES GARLIC, PEELED
LEMON OIL (A GOOD QUALITY OILIVE OIL INFUSED WITH LEMON ZEST)
3 LB CHICKEN, DEBONED AND CUT IN HALF WITH BREAST, THIGH AND LEG ATTACHED
2 TSP DICED SHALLOTS
200 ML HEAVY CREAM
1 LB SPINACH, WASHED AND TRIMED

Heat the olive oil in a large skillet, and sauté the diced mushroom and vegetables until wilted. Set aside to cool. When the vegetables are cooled, mix with the crème fraiche or sour cream, wild rice and herbs. Place half of the mixture in the centre of each pastry round. Egg wash the edges and fold together, forming a "Cornish Pasty" shape. Crimp the edges well, and set turnovers aside. In a 250°F oven, gently roast the garlic cloves in lemon oil until soft but not brown, approximately 1 hour. Remove from the oven and set aside. Set a heavy-bottomed cast iron pan onto medium high heat, add a little lemon oil and place the chicken halves skin side down. Cook for 5 minutes until the skin begins to brown. Pour off some of the fat. Place a couple of heavy pans on top of the chicken, press firmly and place in a 350°F oven for 8-10 minutes or to desired doneness. When the chicken is placed in the oven, put in the turnovers as well and bake until golden brown. While the chicken is cooking, sauté the diced shallots in a sauté pan, add the cream and allow the sauce to reduce until thick. Add the spinach (make sure spinach is fully dry when added or it will thin the cream too much). To serve, spoon the spinach onto two plates and place the chicken on top. Add the turnovers on top of the chicken, spoon four garlic cloves around each and drizzle some lemon oil on top.

*Pâté Brisée (Food Processor Method)

Makes enough for 4 turnovers.

1 C FLOUR
4 TBSP (½ STICK) BUTTER, FROZEN, CUT INTO SMALL PIECES
⅛ TSP SALT
1 TBSP LEMON JUICE
1 EGG

Put the metal chop blade in place in the food processor's beaker. Put the flour, frozen butter and salt in the beaker, and process for 8-10 seconds, using the on and off method, until the butter is cut into the flour and the mixture forms very small flaky granules. Add the lemon juice and egg and process until a ball of dough forms on the blade (about 15 seconds). The dough should be damp but not sticky. If it seems too soft, sprinkle it with 1-2 tablespoons of flour and process for an additional 5-6 seconds. If it seems too dry, sprinkle with a few drops of water and process until well combined. Remove the ball of dough, wrap in wax paper or foil, and chill until firm but still malleable.

POINT NO POINT RESORT

1505 West Coast Road
Sooke V0S 1N0
Tel: 646-2020
Fax: 646-2294
www.pointnopointresort.com
Certified Organic
West Coast Seafood
Owners: Sharon and Stuart Soderberg
Chef: Jason MacIsaac

Open year-round, daily for lunch (11:30 am to 3:00 pm) and afternoon tea (2:30 to 4:30 pm); dinner served February 10 to December 31 (5:30 to 9:00 pm)

I have always loved the name, and have made many visits over the years for the delicious cinnamon toast and carrot cake served at afternoon tea. Other people I know have enjoyed the little woodland cabins, perfect rustic retreats from the city beat. Today, Point No Point Resort still claims one of the most breathtaking views on Vancouver Island. The restaurant and cottages, now significantly upgraded, draw an international set together with sentimentalists like myself.

Chef MacIsaac is constantly seeking out excellent sources for organic produce in the area. "Quality must start with the basics. The finest food begins with the finest ingredients," says MacIsaac, who delights in the quality he finds at Sooke's ALM Organic Farm and Metchosin's Single Hill Farm.

A self-described "surfer and punk rocker with a tremendous enthusiasm for food and wine," MacIsaac's interest in organics stems from the time he spent working at Victoria's Café Brio. He feels that working with organic farmers and their high quality products supports the local community as a whole.

SALAD OF ARUGULA, BABY BEETS AND SALT SPRING ISLAND GOAT CHEESE WITH AN ORANGE VINAIGRETTE AND WALNUTS

Jason MacIsaac, Point No Point Resort
Makes 6 individual-sized salads.

2 BUNCHES ARUGULA, LEAVES WASHED, DRIED AND TRIMMED (COVER WITH A TOWEL IF NOT USING IMMEDIATELY)
18-24 BABY BEETS (QUANTITY DEPENDS ON SIZE)
2 150-G CONTAINERS GOAT CHEESE
1 ORANGE, ZESTED, JUICE RESERVED
¼ C WALNUTS, ROUGHLY CHOPPED
¾ C EXTRA VIRGIN OLIVE OIL
¼ C APPLE CIDER VINEGAR
SALT AND PEPPER

Cut the tops from the beets, leaving 2 inches of stem attached to the root. Put the beets in a pot and cover with water by 1 inch. Add 1 tsp salt, bring to a boil and cook gently for 5-10 minutes, until tender enough so that a paring knife will pass through with ease. Be careful not to over cook. Strain the beets and set aside to cool. Make the vinaigrette by mixing together the olive oil, apple cider vinegar, the orange zest, half of the orange juice, and salt and pepper to taste. Divide each container of goat cheese into 3 equal portions so that you have a total of 6 portions. Shape the cheese into small hockey-puck shapes and roll in the chopped walnut to give a generous coating. Refrigerate. Preheat oven to 350°F. When beets have cooled down enough to handle, peel the skin off using paper towel or cloth. Keep the 2-inch stems intact. Put the beets into the vinaigrette to marinate. To plate each salad, arrange ⅙ of the arugula leaves one on top of the other in the 11:00 to 12:00 o'clock position. Spoon out 3-4 beets and place on the plate in a staggered assembly. Put the goat cheese on a metal pan and slide it into the oven for 2 minutes or until

slightly warmed. Remove from oven and place each "puck" at the base of the arugula so it is propped up. Spoon some dressing over the arugula and a small amount over each beet. The juice from the beets will separate from the olive oil, making the presentation simple but very elegant.

SMALL CITY BISTRO

1871 Oak Bay Avenue
Victoria V8X 1P9
Tel: 598-2015
Certified Organic, Transitional and Natural
French Classic Bistro/Eclectic World Cuisine
Owner and Chef: Dave Fallis

Open Monday to Friday, 11:30 am to 3:00 pm, Monday to Saturday, 5:00 to 10:00 pm

I'm always impressed when a restaurant can turn out latkes almost as well as my mother (obviously, no one can ever do better!), and Dave Fallis does a great job. And his potatoes are organic, so what's not to like?

This is a casual bistro with a theatrical décor, and a "keep it simple" philosophy about food. Says Dave, "I let the true flavours and food values speak for themselves. The better and fresher the product, the better the flavour. Whenever possible, I use organic vegetables and free-range meats, as well as wild seafood. Another benefit is that organic foodstuffs generally keep for a longer period of time."

WILD SOCKEYE SALMON WITH WATERCRESS DRESSING

Dave Fallis, Small City Bistro
Makes 2 servings.

1 GARLIC CLOVE
1 SHALLOT BULB
3 BUNCHES WATERCRESS (OR MORE, FOR ADDITIONAL FLAVOUR)
¾ C RICE WINE VINEGAR
¾ C EXTRA VIRGIN OLIVE OIL
PINCH SEA SALT
PINCH FRESHLY CRACKED BLACK PEPPER
2 6-OZ FILLETS WILD SOCKEYE SALMON
SPRIGS OF WATERCRESS, TO GARNISH

CULTIVATED DINING

Preheat oven to 400°F. Blend all ingredients except the salmon in a blender until smooth. In a skillet, lightly sear the salmon fillets, then roast in oven until medium rare, 5 to 8 minutes, depending on thickness. Remove the salmon from oven, and let rest for 2 to 3 minutes. To serve, place salmon on top of desired starch (mashed potatoes, rice or pasta), and ladle 3 to 4 ounces of the watercress dressing over top. Garnish with fresh watercress.

SOOKE HARBOUR HOUSE

1528 Whiffen Spit Road

Sooke V0S 1N0

Tel: 642-3421

Fax: 642-6988

www.sookeharbourhouse.com

info@sookeharbourhouse.com

Organic

Pacific Northwest

Owners: Frederique and Sinclair Philip

Head Chef: Edward Tuscon

Open for dinner daily from 5:00 pm.

A charming clapboard inn perched at the water's edge in Sooke houses one of the world's best gourmet restaurants. Its enviable reputation has been sealed many times over with accolades and awards from *Gourmet*, *Condé Nast*, and *Bon Apétit*, to name a few. Recently, the restaurant's wine collection earned one of the Wine Spectator's rare Grand Awards.

Go for dinner, and you can't help but join in the praise. On your arrival, the lovely kitchen gardens beckon, with some 400 varieties of vegetables, herbs and edible flowers, and gardeners happy to answer your questions. The gardens are an integral part of the dining experience here, as the menus revolve around their bounty, together with fresh local organic seafood, meat and produce.

Step inside, and the natural setting seems to follow. Large windows let the sun and gardens in, and the décor is a cheerful composition of art and antiques. As you are warmly greeted, spectacular gastronomic preparations are afoot behind the scenes! You will dine on extraordinary creations by Edward Tuscon and his talented young brigade, inevitably eating things for the first time that you would never imagine were

harvested locally. A dinner here will be imprinted on your memory forever, especially when followed by a stay in one of the inn's 27 unique and luxurious guestrooms (did I mention the breakfast in bed to end all breakfasts in bed?).

Sinclair Philip is a charming and gracious man, who has shared his knowledge and enthusiasm for local organic food with his patrons and the public alike. He has worked closely with the noted ethno-biologist Nancy Turner, to bring indigenous plants to his restaurant's menus, and is an avid supporter of Farm Folk/City Folk and the Island Chefs' Collaborative.

WILLIE'S BAKERY AND MARKET CAFÉ

537 Johnson Street
Victoria V8W 1M2
Tel: 381-8414
Fax: 381-8415
www.isabellasbb.com/willies
Certified Organic, Transitional and Natural
Bakery Café
Owners: Shellie and Mike Gudgeon
Baker: Michael Van Dyke

Open daily, Monday to Friday, 7:00 am to 5:00 pm, Saturday to Sunday, 8:00 am to 5:30 pm, later closings in summer

Willie's Bakery and Market Café has returned to its original location in Victoria, after a century's absence. The modern Tuscan interior looks surprisingly comfortable in this 1887 Victorian building. If time allows, it's great to soak up the atmosphere inside with some locally roasted, organic San Juan coffee and straight-from-the-oven croissants, muffins, danishes or cookies. In summer, it's de rigueur to take your coffee on the brick patio by the charming fountain, although heaters allow this year-round. Full breakfasts and soup-and-sandwich lunches are available, and freshly baked baguettes walk out the door all day long.

Formerly sous chef at The Marina Restaurant and Café Brio, Michael Van Dyke says he uses "the best ingredients we can find in season with an emphasis on fresh and local. I always try to support the local farmers as best I can, particularly for fruit and the vegetables for our soups and sandwiches. My emphasis is always to get as close to the source as possible, so that I know what I'm getting." One very close source is

Michael's organic potted herb garden, located just outside the bakery's kitchen door.

I first heard about the famous French toast from Michael's wife, Deepo, of Ollek Farms, who supplies the naturally grown sweet strawberries that complement this dish in summer.

WILLIE'S FAMOUS FRENCH TOAST WITH MASCARPONE AND FRUITS

Michael Van Dyke, Willie's Bakery and Market Café
Makes 2 generous servings.

Toast

1 LOAF RAISIN RYE BREAD OR SIMILAR
1 C WHIPPING CREAM
1 C LIGHT CREAM
2 TBSP PURE VANILLA EXTRACT
PINCH OF NUTMEG
PINCH OF CINNAMON
¼ C MAPLE SYRUP
BUTTER, AS NEEDED

Sauce

1 C MASCARPONE
½ C WHIPPING CREAM
½ C MAPLE SYRUP

Fruit

SLICED STRAWBERRIES, RASPBERRIES, BLUEBERRIES, OR SAUTÉED APPLES – WHATEVER IS IN SEASON

Thickly slice the bread, allowing 2-3 slices per person. Set aside. Prepare the sauce by whipping the mascarpone and whipping cream in an electric mixer or food processor until fully combined. With the motor still running, drizzle in the maple syrup. Set aside. In a mixing bowl, combine the eggs, whipping cream, light cream, vanilla, nutmeg, cinnamon and maple syrup. Immerse the bread slices in this mixture, letting them sit for 2 minutes to fully soak it up. Melt the butter in an oven-proof skillet, and sauté the toast until golden. Flip the toast over and finish it off in the oven, baking until a nice golden brown. To serve, place the toast on a plate, drizzle over the sauce and top with fruit and a sprig of mint.

ZAMBRI'S

#110-911 Yates Street
Victoria V8V 4X3
Tel: 360-1171
Fax: 413-3231
zambris@home.com
Certified Organic and Natural
Spaghettaria by day, Italian restaurant by night!
Owners: Jo and Peter Zambri

Open Monday to Thursday, 11:00 am to 7:00 pm, Friday, 11:00 am to 4:00 pm and 5:00 to 9:00 pm, Saturday, 11:00 am to 4:00 pm and prix-fixe, reservation-only dinners. Take-out items always available.

In a word, Zambri's cooks. When siblings Jo and Peter opened their small restaurant in a somewhat obscure location last year, their noble intention was to bring real Italian cooking to Victoria. Well, Victoria never ate so well! Their success was instant, and Zambri's has become a meeting place for, most tellingly, other Victoria chefs and foodies.

Peter is the chef, as thoughtful and modest as you would want the man preparing your Penne with Smoked Salmon and Peas or Veal Shank with Gorgonzola Sauce to be. His idyllic career has included stints in Italy, at Toronto's Windsor Arms Hotel, the Wedgewood Hotel in Vancouver, Château Whistler and the exemplary Sooke Harbour House, where he both cooked and gardened, developing their highly efficient organic composting system. He once took a year off to pot, and hopes one day to make all the dishes for his restaurant.

Jo is warm and welcoming, remembering everyone's name and favourite dish. Their family grew up in Toronto, always growing and eating produce from their own garden. Jo is genuinely concerned that "we are the first generation not to eat organic foods naturally," that we have to make a special effort to eat the healthy food our parents and grandparents took for granted.

The restaurant buys produce from ALM Organic Farms, ProOrganics, Fairburn Farm and others, and Peter regularly shops at the Saanich farm gates. He eats mostly organics personally, preferring food "grown by someone who knows what they're doing versus mass production."

Zambri's Saturday-night prix-fixe suppers are the ultimate expression of Italian hospitality and fine food, and remind me of the old Tricolore family-style dinners of a decade ago.

PASTA AND FAGIOLI* SOUP

Peter Zambri, Zambri's
Makes 4 servings.

250 G DRIED WHITE BEANS
¼ C OLIVE OIL
1 SMALL ONION, CHOPPED
1 STICK CELERY, IN MEDIUM-SIZED DICE
6 C WATER OR VEGETABLE BROTH
SALT AND FRESHLY GROUND BLACK PEPPER
2 SMALL TOMATOES, PEELED, SEEDED AND CHOPPED
1 CLOVE GARLIC, CHOPPED
200 G SMALL PASTA (DRIED)
SMALL HANDFUL OF PARSLEY
GRATED PARMESAN (PREFERABLY PARMIGIANO-REGGIANO)
OLIVE OIL

* the Italian word for beans, usually white kidney beans

Soak the beans overnight, completely covered in water. In a medium-sized pot, heat approximately ¼ cup of olive oil and incorporate the chopped onion and celery, and cook until soft. Drain the beans of the soaking water, and put them in the pot with the vegetables. Cover with the 6 cups of water (or better, vegetable broth) and cook covered for about one hour; then season with a good dose of salt and pepper. Continue cooking until the beans are completely cooked (about 2 hours). Add the chopped tomato, garlic, and pasta, and cook until the pasta is cooked through. When plating the soup, use hot bowls and garnish with the chopped parsley, grated Parmesan cheese, and a drizzle of olive oil.

JENNY CAMERON, PERSONAL CHEF

1330 Mt. Newton Cross Road
Saanichton V8M 1S1
Tel: 544-1780
Fax: 544-1185

decrone@pacificcoast.net
Certified Organic, Transitional and Natural
Personal chef-caterer
Owner: Jenny Cameron

Available year-round

Best-selling cookbook author, cooking teacher and personal chef-caterer, Jenny Cameron believes that "when produce and meat are local and organic, you know specifically what the composition of your food is." Jenny grew up with farm-fresh ingredients all around her at Ravenhill Herb Farm, and insists that fresh also means flavourful. "When I eat an organic ripe strawberry, raw fresh asparagus, or buttery, nutty arugula, it is difficult to acquire a taste for anything less."

"I use an abundance of fresh herbs, greens and edible flowers from our organic herb farm, together with local organic produce and meat whenever possible," says Jenny. "I suggest menus that reflect the season and then tailor them to my clients' taste. My menus have French, Italian and Asian influences, using less fat and more fresh herbs, good olive oil, garlic, lemons, limes and vinegars — beautifully presented and, of course, absolutely delicious!"

The following recipe is reprinted with Jenny's permission from *Herbal Celebrations* cookbook by Noël Richardson and Jenny Cameron (Whitecap Books, 2000).

STRAWBERRIES WITH MINT AND LEMON VERBENA

Jenny Cameron, Personal Chef
Makes 4-6 servings.

- 4 C FRESH STRAWBERRIES, GENTLY WASHED AND HULLED
- 2 TSP FRESH LEMON JUICE
- 1 TSP FINELY CHOPPED FRESH LEMON VERBENA
- 1 TBSP FINELY CHOPPED FRESH MINT
- ½ TSP MINCED FRESH GINGER
- 1 TBSP SUGAR
- 1 TBSP FINELY CHOPPED FENNEL FRONDS

Toss all ingredients together and serve in individual glasses or in one large glass bowl.

CHERYL'S GOURMET PANTRY
2009 Cadboro Bay Road
Victoria V8R 5J4
Tel: 595-3212
Fax: 595-1294
Natural
Full-service catering; retail outlet
Owner: Cheryl Schultz

Open year-round, Monday to Saturday, 10:00 am to 7:00 pm

When Cheryl opened the first high-end fine food shop and catering company, it felt like Victoria had come of age. Suddenly, it was possible to have seriously catered dinner parties, deluxe take-outs, and even customized hampers for picnics *à deux*. I served Cheryl's salmon pâté on my own china so many times, I finally had to admit to pleading guests that it wasn't actually my recipe!

Cheryl uses "about 80% local organic produce during summer and fall, and as much as we can throughout the year. We strongly support our local farmers." Among those farmers are Hazelmere Farms and Smyth Farms. All her seafood is wild, and organic meat and poultry can be requested. On the shelves is a unique collection of condiments, with many organic options.

"I think it is very important to use locally grown organic produce whenever possible, even if it means paying a little more as in the long run it all comes back to us in the form of a stronger and healthier local economy," says Cheryl. "In recent years, our clients have also come to appreciate the fact that we are strong supporters of local and organic." She believes the demand for organics in the catering business comes through her clients' personal use, and says there is no question that organic products sell better.

GRILLED LEMON DIJON SALMON
Cheryl Schultz, Cheryl's Gourmet Pantry
Makes 4 servings.

4 6-OZ FILLETS OF WILD SALMON

Marinade

¼ C MAYONNAISE
2 TBSP DIJON MUSTARD

JUICE OF 1 LEMON
4 TBSP CHOPPED FRESH DILL
1 TSP SEA SALT
1 TSP FRESHLY CRACKED BLACK PEPPER

Mix together all marinade ingredients. Coat the salmon fillets with the marinade, and allow them to sit at room temperature for 20 minutes. On a high heat, grill the salmon for 5 minutes per side or until done.

CONSCIOUS KITCHEN AND CONSCIOUS KITCHEN COOKS!

2594 Penrhyn Street
Victoria V8N 1G3
Tel: 721-5961
Cell: 514-1544
consciouskitchen@home.com
Certified Organic, Transitional and Natural
Cook service and cooking classes
Owner: Laura Moore

By appointment

Laura Moore says her mission is to "assist and support people to make the transition to a whole-foods, health supporting diet." She accomplishes this through her informative, hands-on cooking classes, and through a private cook service.

She has taught a month-long cooking class that gives students both a practical education about whole-foods ingredients, and the opportunity to really get involved with gourmet vegetarian whole-foods cuisine. These sets of four, two-hour workshops are taught at Fairfield Community Centre. In the second week, Laura steers students through a two-hour tour of Capers Community Market for an in-depth education and exploration of the products and ingredients available there.

Conscious Kitchen Cooks! is Laura's personalized cook service, providing wholesome gourmet vegetarian meals on a weekly or bi-weekly basis. In order to prepare a week's worth of meals for each of her clients, Laura keeps track of what they have in their cupboards, develops unique menu plans, shops for fresh ingredients, and finally, cooks up a storm in each client's home to prepare the food. Clients come home to that evening's meal and a freezer full of entrees for the week ahead.

CULTIVATED DINING CATERERS

"My motto is 'intensely delicious — densely nutritious'!" says Laura. "In the whole-foods, vegetarian cooking classes I teach, I emphasize maximizing the nutritional values and effects of foods, and utilize organic ingredients and a wide variety of alternate whole grains and flours in naturally low-saturated fat, dairy-free recipes."

Laura has been developing recipes for Fresh Piks Organics since 1998, and will be developing hemp recipes for the Trans Global Hemp Company.

COCONUT CURRIED POTATO, SPINACH AND CHICKPEAS

Laura Moore, Conscious Kitchen
Makes 4 servings.

1½ C BROWN BASMATI RICE
3 C FILTERED WATER
1 VEGETABLE BOUILLON CUBE
2 TSP SPANISH SAFFRON
1½-2 RED OR RUSSET POTATOES, CUBED
1 C LEEKS, CHOPPED
1 C ONIONS, DICED
1 TBSP SESAME OIL OR COCONUT BUTTER
1-2 TBSP CURRY PASTE — MILD, MEDIUM OR HOT; YOUR CHOICE!
1 CAN COCONUT MILK (REGULAR, NOT LIGHT)
1 BUNCH SPINACH, WASHED, SPUN DRY AND CHOPPED
1 CAN CHICKPEAS
TOASTED SESAME SEEDS AND/OR CHOPPED CILANTRO TO GARNISH

Measure the rice into a medium-sized saucepan. Add the water, bouillon cube and saffron. Bring to a boil, stir once, cover with a fitted lid and reduce heat to simmer. Cook for 45 minutes. Place potato cubes in a steamer basket and steam over medium heat for 18-20 minutes. Remove from heat and rinse with cold water. Allow the potatoes to cool to room temperature. Place a medium-sized frying pan over medium-high heat. Heat the oil, add the leeks and onions, and sauté until golden and caramelized (8-10 minutes). Add the curry paste to the caramelized onions and leeks, and mix in well. Pour the coconut milk into the frying pan, mix in and simmer for 20-22 minutes over very low heat, allowing sauce to reduce. Place the chopped spinach in pan with the sauce. Cover and let sit 2-3 minutes. Remove lid, fold softened spinach into the sauce and remove pan from the heat. In a large mixing bowl, fold together the sauce, steamed potatoes and drained chickpeas. Serve the curried mixture on a bed of the saffron rice, and garnish with the sesame seeds and/or chopped cilantro.

CUISINE WITH HEART
Victoria
Tel: 595-3310
e_melling@hotmail.com
Certified Organic
Full-service small-scale catering
Owner: Liz Melling

By appointment

L iz is both a counsellor and a cook, and her two vocations happily intertwine. She feels that "being aware of the quality of the food that I use in catering enables me to nourish and nurture people to the best of my ability."

That nourishment might be just-picked organic greens with an orange vinaigrette, followed by seafood in puff pastry, and pear and apple tart, which happens to be a menu I enjoyed at a luncheon catered by Liz.

"I carefully choose menus that appeal to all senses," says Liz. "Depending on the season, finding and using good quality produce is important."

MEXICAN RICE AND BEANS

Liz Melling, Cuisine with Heart
Makes 6 servinigs.

   2 TBSP OLIVE OIL
   1 ONION, CHOPPED
   1½ C SLICED MUSHROOMS
   2 SWEET PEPPERS (GREEN, YELLOW, ORANGE OR RED OR COMBINATION),
   CHOPPED
   2 CLOVES GARLIC, MINCED
   1 CAN (28 OZ) WHOLE PEELED TOMATOES, UNDRAINED
   1 CAN (19 OZ) KIDNEY BEANS, DRAINED (OR SUBSTITUTE OTHER BEANS)
   ¾ C FILTERED WATER
   ¾ C LONG GRAIN BROWN RICE
   1 TBSP CHILI POWDER
   2 TSP CUMIN
   ¼ TSP CAYENNE PEPPER
   1 C CHEESE (MOZZARELLA, ASIAGO, PARMESAN OR YOUR CHOICE),
   SHREDDED

Heat oil in large skillet or Dutch oven. Add onion and mushrooms, and cook 3-5 minutes. Add garlic and peppers, and cook 2-3 minutes.

Add tomatoes, beans, rice, water and spices. Cover, and simmer for approximately 25 minutes. Preheat oven to 350°F. Transfer mixture to a large baking dish, and sprinkle with cheese. Bake for 15 minutes or until cheese melts.

FEYS & HOBBS: CATERED ARTS INC.

#1-845 Viewfield Road

Victoria V9A 4V2

Tel: 380-0390

Fax: 380-0398

www.feysandhobbs.com

feysandhobbs@home.com

Certified Organic, Transitional and Natural

Full-service caterers

Owners: David Feys and Mr. Hobbs

This is not a retail outlet, but pre-orders can be picked up.

David Feys comes by his expertise with natural food honestly, having worked in the kitchen of Sooke Harbour House. With the quietly famous Mr. Hobbs, he launched his custom catering company six years ago, providing personalized menu planning and catering for "a myriad of client events."

Says David, "Years of working in this area have created a solid network of local farmers to provide seasonal produce, and foragers to supply wild berries and mushrooms. Organic or natural produce is most preferred as it tastes better and has better colour and, often, texture. We work hard to use organic/natural produce, but seasonality issues must be taken into consideration with year-round supply requirements. BC produce is always chosen over imported whenever possible."

David says he "aims to produce the highest quality food, always from scratch, with simple preparations to ensure clean flavours." I remember an elegant luncheon that David catered last Christmas. His aim was indeed met, with nothing missing but the ever-modest Mr. Hobbs.

ROOT VEGETABLE TERRINE

David Feys, Feys & Hobbs: Catered Arts Inc.

Makes 12-16 servings.

Yukon Gold Layer

10 OZ PEELED AND THINLY SLICED YUKON GOLD POTATOES
1 TSP EACH FRESH CHOPPED ROSEMARY AND THYME
2 OZ WHIPPING CREAM
1 OZ GRATED WHITE CHEDDAR
SEA SALT AND FRESHLY GROUND BLACK PEPPER
½ CLOVE GARLIC, FRESHLY GRATED

Beet Layer

5 OZ PEELED AND THINLY SLICED BEETS
1 TSP CARAWAY SEEDS
2 TSP APPLE CIDER VINEGAR
1 OZ WHIPPING CREAM
SEA SALT AND FRESHLY GROUND BLACK PEPPER

Purple Potato Layer
(IF PURPLE POTATOES ARE AVAILABLE, USE, IF NOT, OMIT)

10 OZ PEELED AND THINLY SLICED PURPLE POTATOES
1 TSP FRESH THYME
1 OZ WHIPPING CREAM
½ CLOVE GARLIC, FRESHLY GRATED
SEA SALT AND FRESHLY GROUND BLACK PEPPER

Carrot Layer

10 OZ PEELED AND THINLY LENGTHWISE-SLICED CARROTS
1½ TSP HONEY
2 TSP CHOPPED FRESH TARRAGON
1 OZ WHIPPING CREAM
SEA SALT AND FRESHLY GROUND BLACK PEPPER

Spray a 10" spring-form pan with non-stick spray and lay a large piece of plastic wrap in it to line the bottom and sides. Leave the overhanging plastic, to enclose the top of the terrine before baking. Prepare the vegetables, peeling and slicing the potatoes, carrots and beets and measuring each ingredient as you place it into a layer. Begin with half of the white potato: evenly layer the potatoes in the bottom of the pan. Sprinkle with the cheese, cream, herbs and salt and pepper. Next, half of the purple potato: evenly layer the potatoes and top them with the garlic, cream, salt, pepper and herb. Next, half of the beets: evenly spread the beet slices over the purple potato. Top with the caraway seeds, vinegar, and cheese, and sprinkle with the cream. Now, all of the carrots: evenly spread the carrot slices over the beets. Top with the herb, honey, cheese, cream, salt and pepper. Reverse the order to fill the pan to the top: beets, purple potatoes and lastly, the white potato. Wrap the terrine with the tails of plastic wrap, cover with tin foil and place the spring form

pan on a baking sheet (to catch any juices that may come out). Bake at 350°F for about 1½ to 2 hours, until a knife or skewer inserted into the centre goes in easily, i.e., the vegetables are tender and cooked. Remove the terrine from the oven and put another spring-form pan bottom on the top. Weight the terrine with a couple of tins of tomatoes, and leave it on the baking sheet to collect the juices. Cool slightly and then put it in the fridge to set, overnight if possible. To serve, unwrap and turn the terrine onto a cutting board. Cut into 12 or 16 portions. Place on a baking sheet sprayed with a non-stick spray. Warm for about 20 minutes at 325°F, uncovered.

David's note: "This is a modern and fairly low-fat 'scalloped' dish. It's terrific for a buffet as you make it ahead and even portion it ahead. Reheat in the oven or the microwave. The secret is to thinly slice the vegetables using a mandolin or Japanese slicer. Watch your fingers! The whipping cream helps to bind the terrine together and keeps the cheese from becoming stringy and 'greasy', but is mostly cooked out in the cooking and weighting process. Lastly, this recipe is reduced from a larger (catering) size, so the actual number of layers may vary when you make it."

TRUFFLES CATERING GROUP

#120-1315 Esquimalt Road
Victoria V9A 3P5
Tel: 384-6366
Fax: 388-9430
www.trufflescatering.net
yummy@pacificcoast.net
Certified Organic and Natural
Full-service catering
Owner: Don Calveley
Executive Chef: Genevieve Laplante

Open Monday to Friday, 9:00 am to 5:00 pm, weekend appointments available.

Don Calveley describes his catering company as "highly creative, with a passion for great food and professional, personalized service." He and his team use organic ingredients whenever possible and aim "to consistently surpass client expectations."

Chef Laplante knows from organic, having grown up on an organic farm in the Gulf Islands. She trained locally, completed her apprenticeship at

the Union Club in Victoria, and then honed her considerable talent in Zurich under Master Chef Hans Jorgen Smolinsky. Back on the west coast, she worked in Los Angeles, then in Vancouver at Moustache Café and The William Tell, before taking over the kitchen at Truffles.

Genevieve loves the daily dynamic of combining her varied cooking background "and those of my staff with the bountiful products the region has to offer, to create exciting menus for Truffles Catering. We are surrounded with some of the most exquisite organic products and I'm proud to show them off to visitors from other parts of the world."

MIXED ORGANIC GREENS, DAIKON AND CHERRY TOMATO SALAD WITH APRICOT BASIL VINAIGRETTE

Genevieve Laplante, Truffles Catering Group
Makes 4 individual-sized servings.

Salad

6 OZ MIXED GREENS (SUCH AS: MUSTARD GREENS, LOLLO ROSA, RED LEAF, FRISÉE, ARUGULA, LAMB'S LEAF, MIZUNA)
1 C SHREDDED DAIKON
½ PINT CHERRY TOMATOES

Garnish

CHIVES
EDIBLE FLOWERS (SUCH AS: CALENDULA, BORAGE, JOHNNY JUMP UPS AND SWEET VIOLETS)

Vinaigrette

6 FRESH, PLUMP, SWEET APRICOTS
½ C MIRIN*
5 TBSP RICE WINE VINEGAR
4 LEAVES FRESH BASIL, CUT IN RIBBONS (*CHIFFONNADE*)
3 TBSP EXTRA VIRGIN OLIVE OIL
SALT AND FRESHLY CRACKED BLACK PEPPER

* a Japanese sweet wine made from glutinous rice, available in many grocery stores and specialty food stores

In a food processor, blend the apricots, mirin, rice wine vinegar and *chiffonnade* of basil. With motor running, add the olive oil in a steady slow stream to emulsify. Adjust the seasoning with salt and pepper.

To serve, arrange the mixed greens on a plate. Layer the daikon and cherry tomatoes over the greens. Sprinkle with the chopped chives and edible flowers. Drizzle with the salad dressing.

Genevieve's note: "This recipe is a celebration of summer! We use organic edible flowers to give a confetti-like finish to the salad. Our salad greens come from a local organic farmer who learned organic gardening from her father on Salt Spring Island. Mrs. Calveley, our proprietor's mother, grows and supplies us with fresh herbs and organic edible flowers for most of the spring, summer and fall."

Chapter Seven: Home Harvest

SEEDS AND PLANTS FOR YOUR OWN ORGANIC GARDEN

> "All of life will be either healthy or unhealthy, according to
> the fertility of the soil."
>
> *(Man, the Unknown*, Dr. Alexis Carrel, 1935)

Organic gardening is nothing new; it's just getting a lot of attention these days. Many people, especially those born after 1946 when fertilizers and pesticides came along, were inadvertently exposed to inorganic produce, and have since become aware of harmful effects, to both the ecosystem and the human system.

The decision to go organic in your own garden means building contaminated soil back up to its original, clean state; introducing natural pest controls such as predator insects or companion planting; choosing sturdy, companionable plants and seeds that are suited to your soil type; planting according to their requirements (sun, shade, wind); and rotating edible crops annually. You'll need to add to your tool shed things like traps and shields for pests, and it will definitely take more muscle and sweat than conventional farming, but ultimately, you will be doing the right thing for yourself, your family, and the planet.

If you are just starting your organic garden, you will probably want to get some advice from the experts. I haven't yet met an organic grower who wasn't willing to answer questions, and there are many interesting seminars and courses on offer (try Mary Alice Johnson and Tina Fraser's organic gardening class at Camosun College or Carolyn Herriot's seminars at The Garden Path Nursery).

Once your garden is ready for planting, it's important to buy sturdy plants that have been open-pollinated, as their seeds will grow identical plants. Avoid hybrid plants, whose seeds will generate plants nothing like the parent. Many growers in the area collect their own seeds to keep the sustainable cycle going. The ones mentioned here are actively selling seeds, and they are all great sources of information for those wanting to start home gardens.

FULL CIRCLE SEEDS

P.O. Box 807
Sooke   V0S 1N0
Tel: 642-3671
fullcircleseeds@yahoo.com
Certified Organic
Vegetable, herb and flower seeds
Owners: Mary Alice Johnson and Tina Fraser
Orders by phone or email

In addition to running ALM Organic Farm, direct restaurant sales, her box program and her stall at the Moss Street Market, Mary Alice Johnson started Full Circle Seeds in collaboration with Tina Fraser from Lynburn Farm in 1994. Open-pollinated, heritage varieties of seeds are collected from flowers, herbs and vegetables at the two farms.

At first the women were collecting seeds for their own farms, and then came the idea to package them for others. Mary Alice believes in "preserving the heritage seeds and develop new strains" and she has some fascinating examples. ALM Organic Farm was originally a turnip farm, so she has stabilized the "Harris Turnip" seed. Recently, a purple osaka mustard plant became crossed with something else, and she is working towards stabilizing the exotic result.

THE GARDEN PATH NURSERY

395 Conway Road
Victoria   V9E 2B9
Tel: 881-1555
Fax: 881-1304
www.earthfuture.com/gardenpath
Natural
Plant and seed nursery
Owner: Carolyn Herriot

Open April, May and June, daily, 10:00 am to 5:00 pm. Carolyn's "Seeds of Victoria" also available at Dig This in Victoria.

Ten years ago, Carolyn Herriot masterfully took control of the overgrown gardens at Victoria's Point Ellice House, returning them — including the dormant kitchen garden — to their original splendour. All the while, she has operated her own nursery and seed business, and

taught organic gardening to both experts and novices like myself. She has an infectious enthusiasm for organic gardening and, like many growers in these parts, generously shares her knowledge.

Carolyn specializes in unusual and old-fashioned varieties of plants that are hard to find commercially. I always feel spoilt for choice at her nursery, such is the vast range of organically grown vegetable plants. In the past few years, she has moved her nursery from a small lot in town to a 2½-acre property on the Saanich Peninsula. Her large demonstration garden includes vegetables, small fruits and herbs, and a mixed herbaceous border.

Carolyn focusses on growing open-pollinated varieties which allow home gardeners to save their own seeds. She sells the well-known "Seeds of Victoria" — flowers, herbs and vegetable seeds from her nursery gardens.

"Knowledge of seed saving is essential for self-sufficiency," says Carolyn. "Collecting seeds completes the food cycle and enables selection of regionally adapted seeds with the traits most valued by the grower — superior vigour, germination and growth from the freshest seeds collected from one's own plants, with no contamination by toxins or genetically modified organisms! I encourage seed saving; when you collect it, you know what's gone into it."

Venture along The Garden Path where morning coffees and afternoon teas are served in Carolyn's rooftop garden, and demonstration workshops are held every Saturday throughout the nursery season. There's a great winter-vegetable plant sale at the end of August/early September (details on website).

HOME HARVEST

THE EASIEST AND MOST DELICIOUS CREAM OF TOMATO SOUP

Carolyn Herriot, The Garden Path Nursery
Makes 2 servings.*

- 1 TBSP BUTTER
- 1 MEDIUM ONION
- 2 C FRESH TOMATOES (ABOUT 10-15 TOMATOES), CHOPPED INTO QUARTERS
- 2 BAY LEAVES
- 1½ TSP SALT
- 1 TSP BLACK PEPPER
- 1 C 2% MILK
- ½ C WHIPPING CREAM
- 2 TBSP SHERRY (OPTIONAL)
- CROUTONS, BASIL SPRIGS OR FINELY CHOPPED PARSLEY TO GARNISH

* for more servings, increase ingredients proportionately (Carolyn often does this for dinner parties)

Sauté onion in melted butter until just soft. Add chopped tomatoes, bay leaves, salt and pepper. Cook on a gentle heat until tomatoes are liquid (15-20 minutes). Remove bay leaves and purée tomato mixture in food processor/blender until smooth.

Stir in dairy ingredients gradually. To prevent curdling, heat slowly and do not allow mixture to come to a boil. Add the sherry if you wish. Serve warm and garnish with either seasoned croutons, sprigs of fresh basil or finely chopped parsley (or all three).

Carolyn's note: "Delicious, quick and easy! My husband [ecologist and author Guy Dauncey] goes nuts over this soup."

VICTORIA'S ANNUAL COMMUNITY SEED SHOW (SEEDY SATURDAY)
For eight years now, locals gather in mid-February at the James Bay Community Centre, 141 Oswego Street, to exchange and purchase organic vegetable, heritage flower, specialty flower and herb seeds. Free workshops and local produce for sale. Tel: 381-5323.

RAVENHILL HERB FARM

1330 Mt. Newton Cross Road
Saanichton V8M 1S1
Tel: 652-4024
Fax: 544-1185
andnoel@pacificcoast.net
Natural
Culinary and some medicinal herbs
Owners: Noël Richardson and Andrew Yeoman

Open April until the end of July, Sunday, 12:00 noon to 5:00 pm

The story of Ravenhill Herb Farm is legendary in these parts. Former Calgarians Noël and Andrew built an herb garden on the Saanich Peninsula and thousands came. And thousands continue to wind their way up the drive to this spectacular ten-acre property with its sweeping views of the Olympic Mountains and Finlayson Arm, and its rambling, inspiring Provençal ambience.

There are two acres of garden, mainly herbs and vegetables, and a delightful barn where herb plants — culinary, landscape and a few medicinal — are set out for sale on Sundays in the spring and summer. Andrew lovingly tends the garden, and dispenses useful growing information to visitors. His *A West Coast Kitchen Garden* (Whitecap Books, 1995) is an authoritative guide to growing herbs and vegetables.

When Noël isn't cooking from the farm's bounty, she is writing — for *City Food, EAT* and *Western Living* magazines. Her *Summer Delights* (Whitecap Books, 1989), *Winter Pleasures* (Whitecap Books, 1990), *In a Country Garden* (Whitecap Books, 1996) and *Herbal Celebrations* penned with daughter Jenny Cameron (Whitecap Books, 2000) all include recipes that use fresh herbs.

Ravenhill Herb Farm hosted Feast of Fields in 1998, and offers a true country Christmas Craft Show in the barn every December.

Noël and Andrew live what they believe: "Feed the soil, plant enough for the bugs and eat seasonally."

The following recipe is reprinted with Noël's permission from *Winter Pleasures* by Noël Richardson (Whitecap Books, 1990).

RED DECEMBER SALAD

Noël Richardson, Ravenhill Herb Farm
Makes 4-6 servings.

1 C COOKED RED KIDNEY BEANS (CANNED MAY BE USED)
1 RED ONION, CUT IN FINE RINGS
1 RED PEPPER, SEEDS AND WHITE FIBER REMOVED, DICED
CITRUS DRESSING (RECIPE FOLLOWS)
1 MEDIUM RED CABBAGE, FINELY SHREDDED
1 C PARSLEY OR CILANTRO, FINELY CHOPPED
GREEN ROMAINE OR SAVOY CABBAGE LEAVES

In a large salad bowl, combine drained beans, red onion and red pepper. Add enough dressing to moisten and set aside to marinate for 30 minutes. Mix in the shredded cabbage, add the remaining dressing and toss well. Sprinkle the top with the chopped cilantro or parsley. To serve, line a large flat dish with green romaine leaves or savoy cabbage leaves and spoon the red salad onto it.

Citrus Dressing

½ C FRESHLY SQUEEZED ORANGE JUICE
2 TBSP DIJON GRAINY MUSTARD
¼ C OLIVE OIL

3 TBSP JAPANESE RICE WINE VINEGAR
¼ C HONEY
3 TBSP POPPY SEEDS
2 SHALLOTS, FINELY CHOPPED
1 TBSP FINELY GRATED ORANGE RIND
FRESHLY GROUND PEPPER

Mix all the ingredients in a bottle with a tight-fitting lid and shake well.

SALT SPRING SEEDS

P.O. Box 444
Salt Spring Island V8K 2W1
Tel: (250) 537-5269
www.saltspringseeds.com
Certified Organic
Seeds — grains, beans, vegetables and herbs
Owner: Dan Jason

Farm visits by appointment only. Seed catalogue on the website, or phone or write for a copy.

Dan Jason believes organics is "the only way to go!" A life-long gardener, he started his seed company in 1987 and has also written and published several books including *Some Useful Wild Plants* (1969), *Living Lightly on the Land* (1998), *Salt Spring Seeds Garlic Book* (with Paul Ingraham), *The Really Whole Food Cookbook* (with Dawn Penny Brooks) and *Save Our Seeds, Save Ourselves* (2000). Just out is *The Whole Organic Food Book* (Raincoast Books, 2001).

Dan says that "considering the present threat to open-pollinated seeds, we are regarding ourselves not only as a seed company but also as a gene bank." His goal is to get his certified organic seeds "to as many people as possible" so that everyone can become self-sustaining.

The following recipe is reprinted with Dan's permission from *Living Lightly on the Land* by Dan Jason (Salt Spring Seeds, 1998).

AMARANTH OR QUINOA PUDDING
Dan Jason, Salt Spring Seeds
Makes 4 servings.

> 2 C AMARANTH OR QUINOA, COOKED
> 1 C APPLE JUICE
> ½ C RAISINS
> ½ C FINELY CHOPPED ALMONDS
> 1½ TSP VANILLA
> JUICE OF ½ LEMON
> GRATED RIND OF 1 LEMON
> DASH OF CINNAMON

Combine all ingredients in a large saucepan, cover and bring to the boil. Reduce the heat and simmer for 15 minutes. Pour the pudding into individual dessert bowls. Top with a few grapes or stawberries and chill.

Dan's note: "This quick and wholesome dessert is also elegant and tasty. It's as light as rice pudding, and much higher in protein."

HOME HARVEST

VALERIE'S ORGANIC SEED GARLIC
6462 Pacific Drive
Duncan V9L 5S7
Tel: (250) 746-7466
hrussell@island.net
Natural
Garlic and garlic seed
Owners: John and Valerie Russell

Open by appointment only. Stall at the New Duncan Farmers' Market.

I met Valerie at the Duncan market and enjoyed her display of the many garlic varieties she grows. When she told me that she would be using the profits from her garlic sales to apply for organic certification, it really struck a chord with me. One small-scale operation at a time, one giant step for the planet. Valerie's small family-owned and -operated farm specializes in many varieties of seed garlic, and they also grow organic herbs and fruits.

"I believe that our food should be grown with our health in mind," says this very committed grower. "What we do to our environment will affect the lives of our children. We must grow our food as organically as possible to help restore environmental balance."

ROASTED GARLIC
John and Valerie Russell, Valerie's Organic Seed Garlic

4 HEADS GARLIC
1 TSP FRESH THYME
1 TBSP OLIVE OIL

Preheat oven to 300°F. Peel the outer skins off the heads of garlic, but leave the cloves attached to the heads. Place the garlic in a small roasting pan. Drizzle with the olive oil and sprinkle with the thyme. Cover and roast in the oven for 1 to 1¼ hours, or until heads are soft. Garlic can be squeezed onto crackers or slices of baguette.

Seeds and/or plants are also available from:

BENSONS' OLDE TYME FARM

DIG THIS, 45 BASTION SQUARE, VICTORIA, TEL: 385-3212

FOREST SPRING FARM

GABRIOLA GOURMET GARLIC

REBECCA'S ORGANIC GARDEN

TWO WINGS FARM

Notes